D0206317

Ancient Oaxaca

This book investigates the emergence of social complexity and state formation in a New World region. Around 500 B.C., the Valley of Oaxaca, in present-day Mexico, was the site of one of the earliest Native American states, when a new regional capital was established at Monte Albán. Today one of Mexico's most famous and spectacular archaeological sites, Monte Albán signaled an important series of changes in regional political structure in the direction of greater political complexity and integration within a larger domain. The four authors of this introductory text have over the years produced much of the most important primary information we have about developing complex societies in this region. Drawing on the abundance of excavated remains and a survey of regional archaeological settlement patterns, they provide a succinct account of the causes and consequences of political change in the region.

RICHARD E. BLANTON is Professor of Anthropology at Purdue University.
GARY M. FEINMAN is Professor of Anthropology at the University of Wisconsin, Madison.
STEPHEN A. KOWALEWSKI is Professor of Anthropology at the University of Georgia.
LINDA M. NICHOLAS is an Honorary Fellow in the Department of Anthropology at the University of Wisconsin, Madison.
All have worked extensively in Oaxaca and have published widely on the archaeology of the region.

Case Studies in Early Societies

Series Editor:
Rita Wright, New York University

This series aims to introduce students to early societies that have been the subject of sustained archaeological research. Each study is also designed to demonstrate a contemporary method of archaeological analysis in action, and the authors are all specialists currently engaged in field research. The books have been planned to cover many of the same fundamental issues. Tracing long-term developments, and describing and analyzing a discrete segment in the prehistory or history of a region, they represent an invaluble tool for comparative analysis. Clear, well organized, authoritative and succinct, the case studies are an important resource for students, and for scholars in related fields, such as anthropology, ethnohistory, history and political science. They also offer the general reader accessible introductions to important archaeological sites.

Ancient Oaxaca

The Monte Albán State

Richard E. Blanton
Gary M. Feinman
Stephen A. Kowalewski
Linda M. Nicholas

CAMBRIDGE
UNIVERSITY PRESS

PUBLISHED BY THE PRESS SYNDICATE OF THE UNIVERSITY OF CAMBRIDGE
The Pitt Building, Trumpington Street, Cambridge CB2 1RP, United Kingdom

CAMBRIDGE UNIVERSITY PRESS
The Edinburgh Building, Cambridge CB2 2RU, UK http://www.cup.cam.ac.uk
40 West 20th Street, New York, NY 10011–4211, USA http://www.cup.org
10 Stamford Road, Oakleigh, Melbourne 3166, Australia

First published 1999

Printed in the United Kingdom at the University Press, Cambridge

Typeset in Plantin 10/12 pt in QuarkXPress™ [SE]

A catalogue record for this book is available from the British Library

Library of Congress Cataloguing in Publication data

ISBN 0 521 57114 6 hardback
ISBN 0 521 57787 X paperback

Contents

Figures

Preface

Our book title, *Ancient Oaxaca*, is well known to students of pre-Hispanic Oaxaca. The original book with this title, edited by John Paddock (1966), stood for many years as the definitive overview of Oaxacan archaeology, and was a book that gave us, and many others, our first taste of this archaeologically exciting region. We dedicate the present volume to John, to keep alive the memory of one of the pioneers of modern archaeology in Oaxaca.

The state that developed at Monte Albán, in the Valley of Oaxaca, Mexico, was the earliest and one of the most influential in pre-Hispanic Mesoamerica. Because of its significance and the richness of its archaeological and epigraphic remains, Monte Albán and the surrounding valley have received much archaeological attention for over a century. Research in the Valley of Oaxaca has included long-term projects that have been among the preeminent investigative efforts in the history of Mesoamerican archaeology. These projects include those of Alfonso Caso and his students and colleagues, and studies by Kent Flannery and Joyce Marcus and their students and colleagues. Our own archaeological settlement pattern surveys of the entire Valley of Oaxaca also have contributed useful data, and we are now extending our survey coverage beyond the boundaries of the valley itself. Although there is still much to do, the amount of information on past social change in Oaxaca is substantial. For the most part, the results of these research efforts are not readily available except in technical and academic publications (Marcus and Flannery 1996 is an important exception). We were therefore delighted when we were invited to contribute a book on Monte Albán to this series.

Rita Wright and an anonymous reviewer provided many useful comments. We are grateful to many persons and institutions who have made it possible for us to work in Oaxaca. The personnel of the Mexican government's National Institute of Anthropology and History (INAH) have graciously provided us with permissions and help of various kinds. Our main source of funding over the years has been the U.S. National Science Foundation. Several universities have provided resources, including the

City University of New York, the University of Arizona, Rice University, the University of Georgia, the University of Wisconsin–Madison, McMaster University, and Purdue University. Lane Fargher, Diane Rowe, and Brook Klink helped to prepare the illustrations and Susan Peters the manuscript. Over the years, we have benefited from the experience and insights of many archaeologists and scholars, among them Kent Flannery, Joyce Marcus, Laura Finsten, Jill Appel, Robert Drennan, Michael Whalen, Henry Wright, Jeffrey Parsons, Marcus Winter, Ignacio Bernal, John Paddock, Donald Brockington, Ronald Spores, Bruce Byland, Elsa Redmond, Charles Spencer, and David Grove. We thank Barbara Metzger for her thoughtful editorial assistance.

1   Introduction: Mesoamerica and its pre-Hispanic civilization

Some 2,500 years ago in the Valley of Oaxaca, in what is now southern Mexico, a profound social and cultural transformation resulted in the region's first state. This polity, centered at Monte Albán, represented a form of government far more complex than any that had developed in the region before. Like only a few other states in the world, it developed in a primary or indigenous context (i.e., without the influence of a preexisting state). Our aim here is to explore how and why this fundamentally new kind of institution developed. Such questions have a long intellectual history, and the origins of primary states remain a key problem for contemporary anthropological archaeology (e.g., Sanders and Price 1968; Service 1975; Wright 1986).

In developing this early state, the pre-Hispanic ancestors of today's inhabitants of the Valley of Oaxaca fashioned an institution that eventually equaled the scale and complexity of other early states in ancient Egypt, Mesopotamia, and North China, as well as other Mesoamerican states such as those of the Aztec and the Maya. Mesoamerica, which includes southern Mexico and adjacent parts of western Central America, was the setting for one of two native urban civilizations in the Americas – the other being the Andean civilization of the Inca and their predecessors.

Through their development of the state as a governing institution, the early inhabitants of the Valley of Oaxaca made a significant contribution to the growth of ancient Mesoamerican civilization. The importance of this contribution should be recognized. But it is not our intention to promote the greatness of one particular society or people. To promote one society or culture always carries the implication that its neighbors were less than great, that they achieved less, that we have less to admire about them, or that we can learn less from them. We study these cultural changes in Oaxaca not because they are entirely unique, but because in some ways they resemble human experiences in other places and in other times. Knowing more about the development of the Monte Albán state helps us understand the causes and consequences of major social transformations in general.

Table 1 *Changes in the Valley of Oaxaca, 600–150 B.C.*

600 B.C.	150 B.C.
Population about 2,000	Population more than 50,000
Largest community San José Mogote, population 1,200	Largest community Monte Albán, population 17,000
Some 80 other settlements, mostly tiny hamlets	Some 643 other settlements, including towns of over 1,000
Regional hierarchy of centers with two levels	Regional hierarchy of civic-ceremonial centers with at least four levels, politically organized as a state
Nearly universal access to farmland with reliable water	Many dependent on rainfall agriculture alone
Settlements confined to the valley itself	Settlements spread into the surrounding mountains
Most of the valley covered with trees	Significant deforestation and erosion around settlements
Several polities in the region, possibly at war with each other	Strong panregional political organization; military outposts suggesting concern with managing the region's boundaries
Tribute minor, symbolic	Tribute in labor and goods required to support state and capital
Status and wealth inequality but no sharp social class difference; possibly social ranking by inherited status	Possibly social stratification, rulers and the ruled
Beginnings of a warfare human-sacrifice complex	Raiding and violence commemorated in monuments; Monte Albán fortified
Ancestor cults	State cult of lightning-clouds-rain
No evidence of canal irrigation	Intensive agriculture, including canal irrigation
Household storage of produce	Some goods possibly acquired through markets
Maize cooked by steaming or boiling	Maize cooked as tortillas using *comales*
Few craft specialists	More craft specialists for basic goods in everyday use
Most houses wattle-and-daub, a few mud-brick	Houses of mud-brick

Many people think that the only great transformation in human society occurred rather recently – the change from a traditional to a "modern" way of life. The simple dichotomies they employ – traditional/modern, primitive/modern, illiterate/literate, preindustrial/industrial, primitive/ civilized – suggest that there have really been only two kinds of cultures or mentalities (Berreman 1978; Service 1975:3). We argue, in contrast, that transformations with tremendous social and cultural consequences for the ways in which people thought and lived occurred many times in the past. Rather than as a singular episode in human cultural evolution, the

---

Box 1 *How archaeologists recognize a state*

Archaeologists and other social scientists define a state as a specialized and hierarchically organized political system that governs society within a particular territory or region. Chiefdoms, also territorial systems of governance, are less hierarchical and less complex (e.g., Service 1975:15–16). Although sources such as Service (1975; cf. Claessen and Skalník, 1978) provide archaeologists with a substantial body of comparative ethnographic and historical data on early states, it is often difficult to use this information as a basis for securely identifying a state on the basis of archaeological data alone. For example, states are often defined as governing institutions that make use of civil law and hold a monopoly of power (i.e., only the state can legitimately make use of violent force to wage war or punish wrongdoers) (Service 1975:14). But these features cannot serve as criteria for recognizing a state where written records are inadequate or absent.

One of the most fruitful methods for archaeological research is one that studies the system of governing places (centers) in a region. Henry Wright and Gregory Johnson (Johnson 1973, 1987; Wright 1969; Wright and Johnson 1975) have argued, on the basis of comparative studies, that states typically have three or more hierarchical levels of centers of governance above villages and hamlets. For example, a large number of low-level governing centers will be found distributed widely across the landscape, each linking a small population of adjacent villages and hamlets to higher levels of government. Groups of these low-level centers will in turn be under the jurisdiction of a smaller number of more important middle-level centers. The major governing center (level three in the regional hierarchy) is the regional capital. Chiefdoms will have only one or two hierarchical levels of centers.

---

modern world is better seen as the product of a complex sequence of transformations in many places over thousands of years. Because contemporary societies have incorporated features from diverse cultural streams and time periods, the social and cultural transformations that occurred in pre-Hispanic Mexico are of considerable interest for the study of cultural evolution and the origins of the modern world.

The transformation we are concerned with here occurred between 550 and 100 B.C. This transition involved many changes, which are listed in Table 1. A prominent aspect of this transformation was the rise of the state (see box 1). This book explains how we determined that these changes occurred, how and why they occurred, and what they tell us about similar episodes of change at other times and in other places.

The transitions that took place over some 400 years had a major impact on most aspects of people's lives, from the everyday habits of domestic life and residence, to the amount and kinds of social interaction that occurred within the region and between regions, to symbolic systems, artistic expression, and public ritual. The major element of social change that precipitated this broad reorganization was the development of an integrated regional polity centered on a newly founded political capital at Monte Albán. In chapters 2 and 3 we discuss the Valley of Oaxaca region and the archaeological research that has provided the information we use, describe Monte Albán's environmental setting, population history, and early architecture, and look at the circumstances that may have resulted in its founding. In chapter 4 we look in detail at the many social and cultural consequences of the new political order, and in chapter 5 we consider it in comparative and theoretical perspectives.

The Valley of Oaxaca was not alone in experiencing profound social and cultural transformation between 550 and 100 B.C. Several contemporaneous societies of Mesoamerica underwent key transitions as well, and what happened in the Valley of Oaxaca cannot be understood apart from this larger domain. Therefore, before we discuss Oaxaca in more detail we need to place it in the context of Mesoamerican civilization as a whole. We begin by discussing the nature of civilizations in general.

The nature of civilizations

In the modern anthropological use of the term (e.g., McNeill 1991; Sanderson 1995), a "civilization" is a large, multicultural society, a type of social system not coterminous with any specific ethnic group or language; civilizations are larger, more inclusive, and culturally diverse. In some cases, a civilization may be dominated or strongly influenced by a particular cultural group; for example, Han Chinese language and culture were central to the development of traditional Chinese civilization. Yet many elements of cultural and linguistic diversity persisted (and continue to the present day) within Chinese civilization (Blunden and Elvin 1983). Even the comparatively homogeneous ancient Egyptian civilization, which grew out of the Gerzean culture of fourth millennium B.C. Upper Egypt, integrated elements from the somewhat culturally distinct Lower Egypt and incorporated populations of Nubians and Libyans (Kemp 1989:ch. 1). These examples illustrate that a civilization is not a particular culture, population, or people, but a large, multicultural system.

The interactions among the diverse cultural groups that participate in a civilizational system are not simply happenstance or random events. Instead, long-distance interactions are essential to the development and maintenance of each local culture (Abu-Lughod 1989; Adams 1974; Curtin 1984; Helms 1988; Schortman and Urban 1992; Wallerstein 1974; Wolf 1982) (see box 2). In civilizations there are regular movements of people, goods, and information across local cultural boundaries. The regularity and intensity of these interactions require specific social institutions (e.g., long-distance traders' associations) and technologies (e.g., domesticated animals or other systems for interregional transport)

Box 2 *World-systems theory*

Traditionally, anthropologists focused their research primarily on local social groups such as neighborhoods, communities, and cultures. Several social scientists writing since the middle of this century have argued that the local cannot be understood apart from a consideration of its place within larger, interactive systems (Wolf 1982). The economist A. Gunder Frank (1969) and the historian Fernand Braudel (1972) were early voices in this movement, but Immanuel Wallerstein (1974) deserves most of the credit for stimulating a flood of research and writing aimed at the development of a more global social science. Whereas Wallerstein studied the growth of the modern (capitalist) world system, others have modified his ideas to make them more directly applicable to noncapitalist situations. As a result, this literature is of interest to archaeologists studying the evolution of early complex societies such as those of pre-Hispanic Mesoamerica (e.g., Abu-Lughod 1989; Blanton and Feinman 1984; Blanton, Peregrine, Winslow, and Hall 1997; Chase-Dunn and Hall 1991b; 1997; Peregrine and Feinman 1996; Schneider 1977; Schortman and Urban 1992).

to make distant interactions feasible and predictable. At the same time, long-distance intercultural interaction is made possible by the sharing of a cultural system or civilizational tradition. This phenomenon can be seen, for example, in the concept of the Oikumene, an area that the ancient Greeks recognized as being occupied by various "civilized" peoples (Kroeber 1952).

In a civilization, many distinctive local cultural systems are systematically linked together into a larger, integrated social and cultural whole – a civilizational tradition that is shared by all the local groups who participate in the encompassing civilization. A civilizational tradition is not simply a combination of the elements of all the local cultures participating in the larger system or the culture of one dominant group. Because it develops out of intercultural interaction, it has many distinctive and new elements. A civilizational tradition to a considerable extent is transcendent, not simply the local writ large. Elements of transcendent culture often include shared ideas about the makeup of the cosmos, a lingua franca, conventions of diplomacy, a common system of weights and measures, a calendar, and a widely recognized "international style" of artistic expression.

A single governmental system rarely covers the whole extent of the larger interactive system of a civilization. Where it does, as happened in some periods of Chinese civilization, we call it a "world empire." More commonly, a civilization is made up of multiple interacting independent polities (an "interstate system" [Chase-Dunn and Hall 1991a]). In these cases, an economic division of labor between the various local cultural groups – a world economy – is the primary basis for long-distance social interactions.

Interaction spheres and world systems

Exchanges of goods across cultural boundaries and a shared, transcendent culture that links disparate local groups are central components of a civilization. Migration between regions is another such component. In another kind of large-scale interactive social system, an "interaction sphere" (Yoffee 1993), goods are regularly exchanged and other social transactions take place across local group boundaries. Each local group participates in the larger interactive system on a nearly equal footing, economically and politically. The South Pacific kula exchange system of the Trobriand Islands, originally described in Bronislaw Malinowski's (1922) *Argonauts of the Western Pacific*, is an example.

By contrast, in early civilizations, as well as in the modern world economy, the patterns of intergroup interaction are hierarchically structured (Chase-Dunn and Hall 1991a). This hierarchical relationship is most evident in differences between cores and peripheral regions. In civilizations powerful core zones extend their influence or domination into peripheral zones in several possible ways. First, populations of the core develop a comparatively centralized political institution – a state. Only states have the power to extend core-zone hegemony and economic influence into peripheral areas. Secondly, the urbanized and comparatively affluent population of a core region, with its powerful ruling groups, state bureaucracy, wealthy merchants, and important temple priesthoods, increasingly finds it necessary to import materials not locally available, including high-value, socially significant prestige and ritual goods. In many cases, these goods are imported from the periphery. As periphery populations are increasingly drawn into this growing multicultural world economy, they become more involved in exchanging their goods or labor for core-zone goods and services (e.g., manufactured items) not locally available to them (Hall 1986). The changes that took place among the eighteenth- and nineteenth-century Plains Indians are a well-documented example of the incorporation of a periphery, in this case into the early modern European world economy (e.g., Kardulias 1990), on the basis of an exchange of furs for European manufactured goods. Cores and peripheries develop in tandem through their mutually reinforcing interactions. The hierarchically structured core-periphery systems of the early civilizations became engines of social, cultural, and technological change as the flows of goods, people, and information across cultural boundaries intensified.

Civilizations do not suddenly spring up fully formed. Each has a lengthy history of development (for example, Frank and Gills [1993] and Gills and Frank [1991] trace the origins of the modern world system back 5,000 years). To introduce the central features of change in the evolution

Table 2 *Time line for Mesoamerica and the Valley of Oaxaca*

	Valley of Oaxaca periods and phases	Mesoamerican periods
1500		Late Postclassic
	Monte Albán V	
1100		Early Postclassic
	Monte Albán IV	
700		
	Monte Albán IIIB	Late Classic
500		
	Monte Albán IIIA	Early Classic
300		
A.D.	Monte Albán II	
B.C.		Late Formative
100		
	Monte Albán Late I	
300		
	Monte Albán Early I	
500		
	Rosario Phase	Middle Formative
700		
	Guadalupe Phase	
900		
	San José Phase	
1100		Early Formative
1300	Tierras Largas Phase	

of Mesoamerican civilization, we first briefly describe it just prior to the advent of extensive European influence (which began with the Spanish conquest) and contrast its form with the situation some 2,500 years earlier, when some of Mesoamerica's distinctive features were just beginning to appear. The development of the state in the Valley of Oaxaca was one of the transformations that provided a foundation for the Mesoamerican civilization of A.D. 1521 (for summaries see Berdan 1982; Blanton Kowalewski, Feinman, and Finsten 1993; Coe 1994; Weaver 1993; Sharer and Grove 1989; Smith 1996a; and Wolf 1959).

Mesoamerican civilization in the Late Postclassic

The final pre-Hispanic period of the Mesoamerican archaeological sequence was the Late Postclassic (table 2). The civilization of the latter part of that period, covering the century or so prior to Spanish conquest,

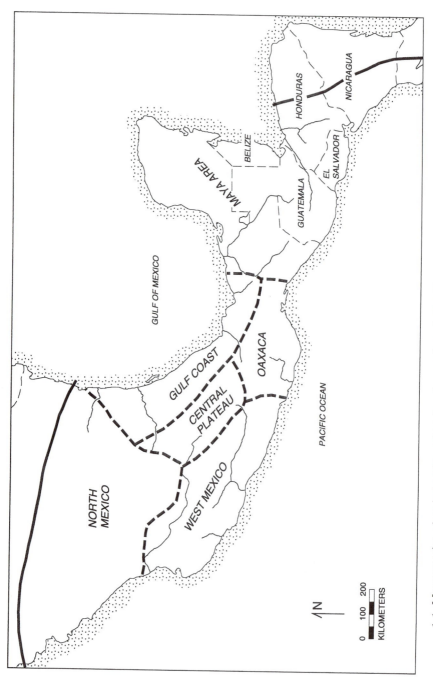

1.1 Mesoamerica, showing major cultural regions and modern nation-states.

extended southward and eastward from central and western Mexico into parts of what are now Honduras, El Salvador, and Nicaragua and all of Belize and Guatemala (fig. 1.1). Within this area of approximately 1 million square kilometers (larger than the area of the U.S. eastern-seaboard states from Maine through Georgia) resided an estimated 35 million people. This vast and populous world economy was environmentally diverse and decidedly multicultural. Its environments ranged from the low-lying wet tropical forest extending from Central America to Gulf coastal Mexico to the rugged mountains of Guatemala and western Mexico; a drier, dissected coastal zone predominated along the Pacific rim. As an indicator of the area's cultural diversity we need only point to its large number of languages, many of them still spoken today. It is estimated that over 200 distinct languages were spoken in pre-Hispanic Mesoamerica, representing some fifteen major language groups (Suárez 1983).

The frequency of intercultural interaction across Mesoamerica was not uniform; by the end of the pre-Hispanic sequence, three major subregions can be detected. Many social interactions, including exchanges of goods, occurred across the fuzzy boundaries of these subregions, and certain key ideas were shared across all of Mesoamerica. To the west was an empire dominated largely by the Tarascan state (Pollard 1993). In central Mexico the Aztec empire, governed by the rulers of the Basin of Mexico capital Tenochtitlan-Tlatelolco (Berdan et al. 1996)(fig. 1.2), extended from the central plateau to both coasts. To the east was the less centrally organized, culturally and physiographically distinctive Maya zone (Sharer 1994). In spite of this partial subdivision and internal variability, Mesoamerica was still a civilization distinct from the societies to the north (including the foraging Chichimecs, considered barbarians by the Mesoamerican peoples) and to the south and east, where there were chiefdoms that lacked many of the distinctive sociocultural features of Mesoamerican civilization.

Material exchanges, migration, institutional arrangements, and transcendent culture linked together the culturally diverse peoples of Mesoamerica. The most salient aspects of this civilization's social and cultural makeup on the eve of Spanish conquest were urbanism, social stratification, political organization, production (including agriculture), specialization and exchange, long-distance interaction, and a civilizational tradition.

Urbanism

Mesoamerica was heavily urbanized. In the core zones a high proportion of population lived in cities (in fact, a higher proportion than in England

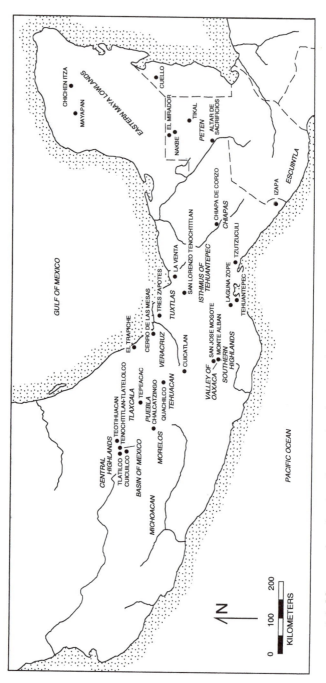

1.2 Mesoamerica, showing places and regions mentioned in the text.

at the same time) (e.g., Berdan et al. 1996:109). In the sixteenth century, scores of cities in the range of 10,000–25,000 inhabitants formed networks in a complex economic and cultural landscape. The Aztec capital of Tenochtitlan-Tlatelolco, with 200,000 persons, was the largest city in A.D. 1521 (Calnek 1976). The growth of core-zone governments, the intensification of commerce in the market plazas, and craft production all combined to stimulate the growth of cities, and these activities were at their most intense in central urban precincts. Mesoamerican cities often centered on broad civic-ceremonial plazas lined by numerous temples, palaces, and other stone buildings erected on top of pyramid-platforms (Marquina 1964) (fig. 1.3).

Social stratification

Everywhere in Mesoamerica, a distinction was made between nobility and commoners. Members of the nobility, who inherited their status, rarely were required to do any productive labor; they often, however, held important administrative or military offices or served in the temple priesthoods. Noble status was evident in their more elaborate housing, attendance of special schools, and consumption of goods such as cotton cloth, sandals, and costly, often exotic items of personal adornment (for central Mexico, see Smith 1996a:ch. 6). Commoners were more restricted in the goods they were allowed to have and were obligated to transfer a portion of what they produced or earned as tribute to the state and to noble landlords. They also were subject to labor obligations enforced by the governing authorities (e.g., Berdan 1982:ch. 3).

Political organization

Governance was carried out for the most part by members of the inherited nobility, but not all areas were governed by states. Particularly in peripheries, local polities often were small (in many cases as few as 10,000–12,000 persons); here each polity was governed by a local noble family (*tlatoani*, in parts of central Mexico) (e.g., Berdan et al. 1996:109), with only minimal development of an administrative hierarchy. Hundreds of these tiny social formations, variously called city-states, petty kingdoms, or patrimonial domains, dotted the landscape (Gerhard 1972). Powerful states developed, however, in the major core zones; the two most prominent ones at the end of the pre-Hispanic sequence were the Tarascan and the Aztec states. The Lowland Maya area had seen centralized states develop during the centuries just prior to the Spanish conquest at the sites of Chichén Itzá and Mayapán, but these had weakened by the

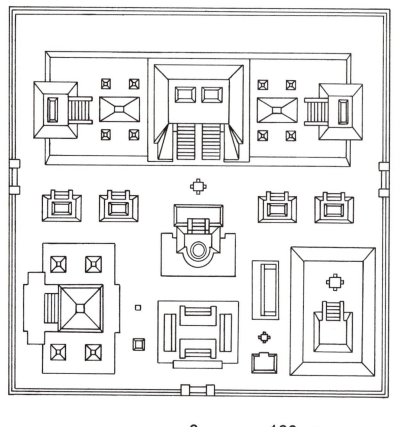

←N—   0   100 m

1.3 Plan view of the central civic-ceremonial plaza of Tenochtitlan, the Aztec capital. Modified from Marquina (1964:pl. 54).

end of the pre-Hispanic sequence, leaving in their wake many small local-ized polities (Andrews 1965; Marcus 1993).

Core states such as the Aztec were governed by renowned rulers (*tecuhtli* in the Nahuatl terminology of central Mexico) who headed expansive domains. The largest of these, the Aztec empire, extending from the Gulf of Mexico to the Pacific Ocean, had grown to include an estimated 9 million persons (Berdan et al. 1996). These rulers dominated vast state administrative systems arranged in several hierarchical levels, including hierarchically structured military establishments, palace retain-ers, and tax collection bureaucracies (Hodge 1996).

CM

1.4 Prestige goods manufactured from shell: beads, pendants, and a bracelet from Oaxaca.

Production

Mesoamerican economies were almost entirely agricultural, with maize, beans, and squash as the major cultigens. Farming in the major core zones was labor intensive and included various forms of irrigation, terracing, fertilization, and lake reclamation (*chinampas*) (see, e.g., Sanders, Parsons, and Santley 1979). States often were involved in the construction and maintenance of such irrigation and lake reclamation projects. The peripheries produced, in addition to the basic food crops, various export products destined largely for consumption in the cores, including cacao (chocolate), cotton, vegetable dyes, rubber, incense, marine shells, jaguar skins, colorful bird feathers, metal implements, and valuable stones such as jade. Such goods as these were more than just fancy consumer items. All over Mesoamerica special things from afar played central symbolic roles in distinguishing nobility from commoners, in displaying accomplishment or military success, in social exchanges with political implications, and as consumables in religious ritual (Berdan 1975; Blanton and Feinman 1984; Brumfiel 1987) (fig. 1.4). These goods were exchanged through tribute and commerce (Berdan 1975).

In addition to agricultural products, Mesoamericans made ceramic

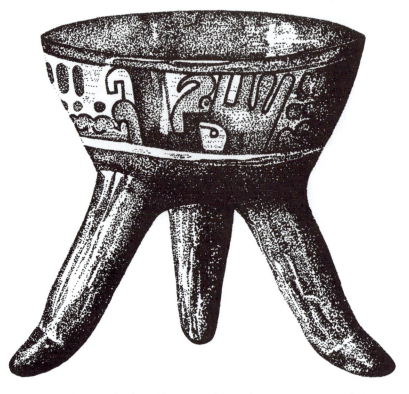

1.5 Pottery in the Mixteca-Puebla style, representative of the cosmopolitan culture of Mesoamerican civilization of A.D. 1500.

vessels, tools, toys, and ritual items such as figurines. Their pottery exhibited a wide range of forms, colors, and techniques; costly pottery of the Mixteca-Puebla international style was renowned for its beauty and was exchanged over long distances (Smith and Heath-Smith 1980) (fig. 1.5). Stoneworking involved technologies such as tunnel mining, heavy quarrying, masonry, sculpture, flintknapping, and delicate lapidary work. Obsidian – volcanic glass – was widely used in tool production and was exchanged all over Mesoamerica, primarily from a few major mines (see, e.g., Spence and Parsons 1972). The products of cotton weaving, the lapidary arts (including jade working), and other exotic crafts involving paper, shell, bronze, gold, and silver, among many others, were destined primarily for ritual and political uses and for elite consumption in the core-zone cities (Berdan 1975). Some utilitarian use was beginning to be made of copper and bronze, particularly in western Mexico, but most metallurgy in Mesoamerica was put to symbolic use (Hosler 1988; Smith and Heath-Smith 1994:359).

Specialization and exchange

Most Mesoamerican households engaged in agricultural production, which itself could be highly specialized. Some households pursued other occupations, including craft production, commercial transactions, transportation, temple service, military service, government administration, and a host of other specializations. Commercial transactions took place in regional systems of periodic markets. These markets offered diverse economic choices to ordinary households but at the same time were of value to political institutions for the tax revenues they produced. The most complex network of periodic markets had developed over a period of many centuries in populous core zones such as the Basin of Mexico (Blanton 1996). Markets specializing in long-distance exchange and "ports of trade" (i.e., market enclaves governed by specialist long-distance merchants) served as nodes in the trade of precious goods between core and periphery (Berdan 1985). In central Mexico, specialist long-distance traders called *pochteca* and *oztomeca* formed guildlike organizations. Much of the long-distance trade in exotic finery was carried out by these merchant institutions (Berdan 1988).

Long-distance interactions

The long-distance movement of people, materials, and information was of considerable importance to core-zone populations and their powerful governments, commercial sectors, and temple priesthoods. The organization of the Aztec capital, Tenochtitlan, for example, allowed for the integration of immigrants – some from distant regions – into the population (Calnek 1978:317). In fact, the immigration of desired craft specialists was encouraged. Several kinds of interregional institutions made possible the regulation of other categories of long-distance interaction. For example, the city of Tepeacac was conquered by the Aztecs and required to develop a new market in which long-distance traders could buy and sell the kinds of preciosities that made up the bulk of long-distance Mesoamerican commerce (Berdan 1980). Goods available here and in similar interregional markets included fine cotton cloth, semi-precious stones, tropical bird feathers, gold, silver, jaguar and ocelot skins, and cacao, among other goods. Long-distance trade required roads, institutions to ensure safe and secure passage, and human porters (*tameme* in Nahuatl). The Aztecs established garrisons to guard their borders and to control routes crucial to both military movement and commercial transactions (Smith 1996b). Additional outposts in conquered provinces served as sites of imperial tribute collection.

The civilizational tradition

Although there were numerous local variations in religious belief and ritual, the Mesoamerican peoples shared many fundamental concepts and practices of religion, cosmology, and ritual (see Nicholson 1971 and Coe 1981). Everywhere the cosmos was viewed as multilayered, with upper and lower worlds between which humans and supernatural beings moved; for example, at death most persons traveled through the levels of the underworld. The lines of the cardinal directions were an additional dimension of cosmic spatial structure; their intersection formed four quadrants that had color and other symbolic significance. The center point, the pivot of the four quarters, or *axis mundi*, was a particularly sensitive location linking supernatural forces to the actions of humans. The directional orientations of public buildings, palaces, and even whole city plans (for example, that of Tenochtitlan) reflected the importance of quadrilateral directionality and pivotal points in approaching and controlling supernatural forces.

Change, metamorphosis, renewal, duality, and the repetitive cycles of time also informed Mesoamerican belief systems. Conflict between deities reflecting the opposing principles represented by warriors and priests was seen as having resulted in the creation and destruction of a succession of worlds. The current world was considered the fifth; four prior cycles had ended in cataclysm as in time would the current one. The movement of the heavenly bodies, especially the sun, the moon, and Venus, reflected the periodic renewal of the world. In particular, the sun's daily movement across the sky manifested the constant struggle between the forces of renewal and destruction. Religious ritual, including bloodletting, offerings, and human sacrifice, was important in ensuring renewal. Rulers both sponsored and participated in these ritual cycles, elevating themselves into the dynamic processes of the cosmos and thereby legitimating the social esteem accorded to them and their worldly control of material resources and politics.

Mesoamerican peoples used two interrelated calendars to trace the passage of time and to structure their ritual cycles. The 260–day sacred calendar resulted from the series of 20 named days with 13 number permutations for each. Every day had directional, color, and other symbolic associations, including favorable and unfavorable prognostications.

Monthly ceremonies were dictated by the symbolic associations of the segments of the sacred calendar. The sacred calendar meshed with a solar-year calendar of 365 days, made up of 18 named months of 20 days each (plus an unlucky 5–day period at the end when it was best to stay at home). Given the differing lengths of the two calendars, the first day and first month of each would occur together on the same day only once every 52 years; this period and its double, 104 years, were significant blocks of time (analogous in some ways to our centuries) and required ritual at their beginning points to ensure that the world would be renewed for another round. As a means of planning and scheduling, the shared calendar was significant in facilitating movement and interaction among Mesoamerica's different regional and linguistic groups.

Dozens of prominent supernatural entities and many more minor ones embodied the various principles of the religious and cosmic system, including sun, moon, femaleness, maleness, youth, old age, priesthoods, political power, warriors, maize, water, lightning, fertility, and dead ancestors. Many of these served as patron gods of cities, temples, or organized groups such as the merchants' guilds. Deities could appear as humans, as animals, or as humans in animal disguise. Priests were responsible for rituals of celestial and earthly renewal and for communicating with the deities and deceased ancestors but could also perform ritual "magic" (including divining, curing, and even witchcraft), while passing between different celestial domains and being transformed alternately into animal and human forms.

Mesoamerica in 1000 B.C.

By the time of the conquest, the people of Mesoamerica had been accumulating, adding, deleting, inventing, emphasizing, deemphasizing, transforming, elaborating, and reworking their symbols and practices for more than 10,000 years. Their civilization was elaborated from a very ancient Native American cultural base. The period we have chosen to illustrate an early phase in the development of Mesoamerican civilization – 1000 B.C. – falls squarely in a portion of the Early Formative period that is sometimes called the Early Horizon (1200 – 900 B.C.). The Formative was the period in which most of the major institutions and cultural features of Mesoamerican civilization were developed (table 2).

A "horizon" is a period in which archaeologists recognize a heightened degree of stylistic sharing and an increase in the quantity of goods moving between regions; the Early Horizon was the first of three such episodes in Mesoamerican history. Accompanying this horizon was the development of a transcendent cultural system that is best known for an art style often called "Olmec" after the region of the Gulf Coast lowlands in which it was first identified (Grove 1997). The Olmec region is not, however, regarded as its heartland (Flannery and Marcus 1994:ch. 20); instead, it combined elements from diverse areas and added to new elements not stemming from any known locality. It was a pan-Mesoamerican phenomenon.

The Early Horizon saw a significant increase in the amount of long-distance interaction over much of Mesoamerica (see, e.g., Grove 1997; Sharer and Grove 1989). Many categories of goods were transported, including obsidian, pottery vessels, pottery figurines, green stone, serpentine, pearl oyster, and marine shell jewelry. Carved jades, magnetite in the form of mirrors, and decorated pottery were important items with special symbolic significance.

Several excavated localities, including Tlatilco in the Basin of Mexico, Chalcatzingo in Morelos, San José Mogote in the Valley of Oaxaca, and San Lorenzo Tenochtitlan in the Gulf Coast lowlands, provide evidence for increasing social differentiation during this time (Flannery 1982). Comparatively elaborate burials and evidence for differential access to exotic material items indicate that status distinctions between households were increasing. In the Gulf Coast lowlands, high-status individuals are featured in monumental portrait stone carvings (Grove 1997).

Many elements of later Mesoamerican religious and cosmological systems were already in use by the Early Horizon. The idea of the four-quartered universe, for example, undoubtedly came to the New World with the first imigrants from northeastern Asia over 10,000 years ago. Even before 1000 B.C., this concept was already undergoing modification for Mesoamerican use, for example, to orient ritual buildings to the cardinal directions (Flannery 1976:334). A complex system of supernatural beings and forces is depicted in various media, including portable stone objects (some in carved jade) and ceramic vessels and figurines. Certain key cosmic and religious principles and supernatural figures were widely recognized (Coe 1989). The art often shows fantastic animals or animal-human combinations. Serpent images, especially a cayman with fire eyebrows, may symbolize sky forces (fig. 1.6, a–c). The were-jaguar is particularly frequent and associated with earth forces (fig. 1.6, d–f). The theme of interrelationships and transformations between animals and humans, a later preoccupation of Mesoamericans, is prominent. Although the societies of 1000 B.C. had not yet developed the sharp distinction between nobility and commoners evident later, the process of social differentiation was nonetheless well under way in several regions, where some individuals made use of their networks of long-distance exchange for their local social advantage. They more than others could

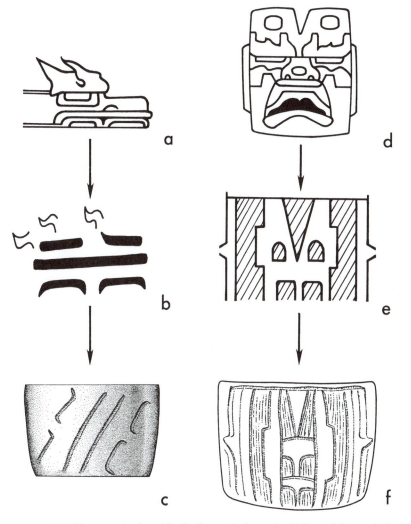

1.6 Fancy carved and incised vessels from the Valley of Oaxaca's San José phase, showing realistic and more stylized versions of the lightning (sky) motif (*a–c*), and the earthquake (earth) motif (*d–f*). Reprinted from Marcus and Flannery (1996:fig. 86). Figure courtesy of Joyce Marcus.

obtain and display the exotic ritual items that were evidently signs of status.

The intensification of long-distance interaction between high-status households that increasingly shared not only ritual items but also cosmological principles, deities, and ritual practices began to create an integrated Mesoamerican world with a transcendent culture. However, little is evident in the way of the division of labor between regions that we see later in the Mesoamerican world-system's core-periphery structure. For example, the major source for magnetite mirrors for a large area extending from the Basin of Mexico to Veracruz was evidently San José Mogote in the Valley of Oaxaca, but the total production enterprise there consisted of only a few households (Marcus and Flannery 1996:102). This small-scale production and exchange does not constitute a core-periphery system. No particular region appears to have economically dominated or conquered others or developed the characteristics of a core zone; for example, there were as yet no cities. The largest community in Mesoamerica at this time may have been San José Mogote, but it was little more than a large village and associated hamlets with a combined population of around 1,000 (Marcus and Flannery 1996:106). Other important sites of the period that served as nodes in exchange networks, such as Chalcatzingo in Morelos and San Lorenzo Tenochtitlan in Veracruz, also had populations estimated at 1,000 or less (e.g., Hirth 1987). Apart from a few households in and around centers that made exotic goods for exchange and status marking, there is little evidence of any pronounced division of labor between households within regions or notable regional specializations in particular export commodities that would have involved the labor of large numbers of households. There were no institutions that could handle large volumes of goods as did the periodic markets and ports of trade of Aztec times.

The importance of states

Mesoamerica was beginning to develop some of its characteristic features by 1000 B.C., but it was still an interaction sphere rather than a civilization. States had not yet developed, and it was states that were instrumental in the intensification of agricultural production, the growth of market systems, craft specialization, and urbanization, and in the increase in the long-distance movement of goods and regional specialization in exports stimulated by tribute flows and commerce.

State formation is a crucial factor in the evolution of Mesoamerican civilization. Three regions, in particular, are known to have been sites of state formation after 1000 B.C.: the Basin of Mexico, probably around

150 B.C. (Cowgill 1992), the Lowland Maya area, beginning between the first century B.C. and the third century, A.D. (Freidel and Schele 1988; Sharer 1994), and the Valley of Oaxaca, just after about 500 B.C. If we are to comprehend the evolution of Mesoamerican civilization, we must examine how the regions that developed states became the core zones of an emerging core-periphery system.

2   The Valley of Oaxaca: a regional setting for an early state

When we speak with the public or beginning students about the pre-Hispanic inhabitants of Mesoamerica, they generally are familiar with the Aztecs, the Maya, and even the great Classic-period central Mexican site of Teotihuacan. There is less recognition of the ancient societies of Oaxaca. This lack of familiarity is somewhat peculiar because the earliest evidence for Mesoamerican writing, dating to 600 B.C., has been found in the Valley of Oaxaca (see box 3). Likewise, Mesoamerica's earliest city, Monte Albán, scenically situated on a 400-meter-high hill at the core of one of Mesoamerica's first states, was founded at the center of the valley around 500 B.C. This early urban center was the capital of a state that endured and remained influential for more than 1000 years.

Archaeologists have long been interested in Monte Albán and its history, antecedents, and surroundings (see Whitecotton 1977). Nineteenth-century archaeological explorers described the famous hilltop city and its carved stones and monumental architectural ruins (e.g., Holmes 1895–97). These pioneers recognized that the glyphs carved on stones at Monte Albán are different from those of the ancient Maya in the eastern lowlands of Mesoamerica. They also noted certain shared conventions between these two sets of hieroglyphs, such as a numerical system in which a bar stood for five and a dot for one.

In the 1920s, the pathbreaking Mexican anthropologist Alfonso Caso first identified the Oaxacan stones as culturally Zapotec, carefully describing the differences between Zapotec writing and that found in other regions (Caso 1928, 1965a and b). During his fifty-year career, Caso established that the ancient Zapotecs of the Valley of Oaxaca developed one of the most powerful and important societies in all of ancient Mesoamerica. By the 1950s he had cleared and reconstructed Monte Albán's Main Plaza. Together with his student Ignacio Bernal, he established the basic ceramic chronology that is still used to date sites in the Valley of Oaxaca (Caso, Bernal, and Acosta 1967). Caso also excavated more than 100 pre-Hispanic tombs, including one of the richest (tomb 7)

Box 3 *Mesoamerican writing*

The earliest evidence for Mesoamerican writing dates to roughly 600 B.C., before either the founding of Monte Albán or the emergence of states in this part of the world (Marcus 1976, 1992). The first Mesoamerican writing that has been preserved appears on carved stones at such sites as San José Mogote (Marcus and Flannery 1996:129–31). Written glyphs on stones from before A.D. 1 have been found along the Gulf Coast and in the highland and Pacific coastal regions of Chiapas. Later Mesoamerican writing systems are best known for four peoples, Zapotec, Mixtec, Aztec, and Maya (Marcus 1992). Records of Mixtec and Aztec writing are composed primarily of late pre-Hispanic texts (or early colonial-period copies of aboriginal texts) written on prepared bark paper or deerskin (see, e.g., Berdan and Anawalt 1997). Most Zapotec writing was preserved on stone. Maya writing, the best known of the four, has survived in a few late pre-Hispanic folding books, or codices, as well as in a large body of texts on stone, pottery, and wall murals from the Classic period. Frequent references to the Mesoamerican calendar led early scholars to believe that the ancient Maya of the Classic period wrote primarily about time and astronomical events. Although time, the calendar, and the cosmos were of great concern to the pre-Hispanic Maya, and other Mesoamerican peoples as well, recent advances in the decipherment of Classic Maya writing have revealed that much of it concerned the recording of dynastic histories, princely accomplishments, and legitimacy to rule.

---

ever found in the Americas (Caso 1969), and published the first systematic study of ancient Zapotec writing and calendrics.

In 1966, Kent Flannery, who earlier had worked in Oaxaca with Bernal's student John Paddock (1966), initiated a research effort, involving specialists from diverse disciplines, on the origins of plant domestication and the transition from mobile hunting-and-gathering lifeways to sedentary farming villages in the Valley of Oaxaca. Primarily through excavations in dry caves and valley floor sites, Flannery and his colleagues provided an abundance of new information relevant to understanding how humans adapted to their environment from the time of the earliest human occupation of the region (roughly 10,000 years ago) until the beginning of Caso's Monte Albán sequence (ca. 500 B.C.) (for summaries see Flannery 1976; Flannery and Marcus 1983; Flannery and Marcus 1994; and Marcus and Flannery 1996). For over a decade, Flannery and Joyce Marcus directed excavations at San José Mogote, the largest center in the Valley of Oaxaca prior to Monte Albán (Marcus and Flannery 1996) (fig. 2.1). Houses, public buildings, and burials were excavated at other pre-Monte Albán settlements in the valley, including Fábrica San José (Drennan (1976), Huitzo (Flannery and Marcus 1983), Santo Domingo Tomaltepec (Whalen 1981), and Tierras Largas (Winter 1972).

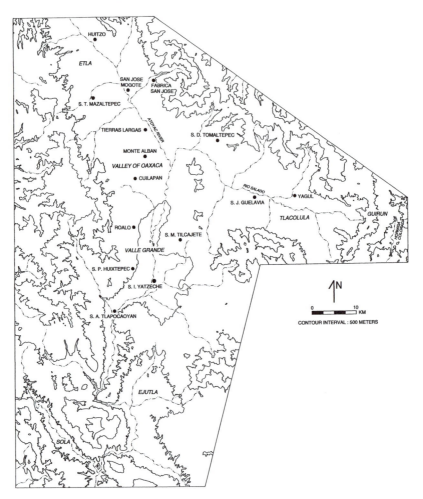

2.1 The Valley of Oaxaca, showing topography, stream drainages, and sites mentioned in the text.

In the 1970s, in cooperation with Flannery's project, his student Richard E. Blanton initiated the systematic surface survey and mapping of archaeological sites in the Valley of Oaxaca. Bernal (1965) previously had located more than 280 large pre-Hispanic sites in the region, reporting many of the area's most significant sites. Blanton (1978) began his more complete and systematic survey by mapping Monte Albán and producing the only complete plan of this ancient urban center (fig. 2.2). Subsequent regional surveys supervised by Blanton and Stephen A. Kowalewski led to full coverage of a 2,150-square-kilometer area that encompasses this large valley and its defining mountain ridges and slopes. Completed in 1980, these surveys recorded more than 2,700 localities with archaeological materials visible on the surface (Blanton, Kowalewski, Feinman, and Appel 1982; Kowalewski et al. 1989). Full-coverage surveys have been conducted in two adjacent and topographically similar regions situated in the central valleys of Oaxaca, the Ejutla Valley, (Feinman and Nicholas 1990a) and the Sola Valley (Balkansky 1997)(fig. 2–3). South of the Ejutla region, Charles W. Markman (1981) completed a survey transect in the Miahuatlán Valley, where small-scale excavations and a reconnaissance had previously been conducted by Donald L. Brockington (1973).

Three mountainous areas that abut the valley also have received full archaeological survey coverage. One of these is the Guirún area (Feinman and Nicholas 1996), running east of the Tlacolula arm of the Valley of Oaxaca almost to the current ethnic divide with the Mixe (fig. 2.4 and box 4). The much larger Peñoles region covers the ridges and slopes between the Etla arm and the Nochixtlán Valley in the Mixteca Alta (Finsten 1996). This region encompasses another current linguistic boundary, that between the Zapotec and the neighboring Mixtec. The third upland area, the Sierra Norte, extends directly north of the Valley of Oaxaca, in the direction of the low-lying Cuicatlán Cañada (Drennan 1989). Collectively, these studies have made the region one of the most completely surveyed areas in the world. They provide a broad perspective and a dynamic record of how human settlement patterns shifted in the period between the establishment of Oaxaca's first sedentary villages and the consolidation of the early state at Monte Albán.

Carved stone monuments are a significant feature of the archaeological record in Oaxaca. As of 1994 some 2,500 were known from the Valley of Oaxaca and surrounding areas, 647 from Monte Albán alone (Urcid 1994; see also Marcus 1992). Many contain brief texts in the ancient Zapotec writing system. These important monuments, generally found in civic-ceremonial contexts, provide a perspective on the ideological conventions associated with the early state in Oaxaca. Other aspects of material culture, including pottery, stone tools, architectural remains, and funerary contexts, offer archaeologists important insights into past lifeways and yield indicators of different patterns of social and economic behavior.

Further insight into these patterns comes from the study of how settlements were situated in relation to the natural environment. An important study of land and water resources in the Valley of Oaxaca by the geographer Anne Kirkby (1973) compared the agricultural yields from different classes of farmland and extrapolated them to the past, taking into account

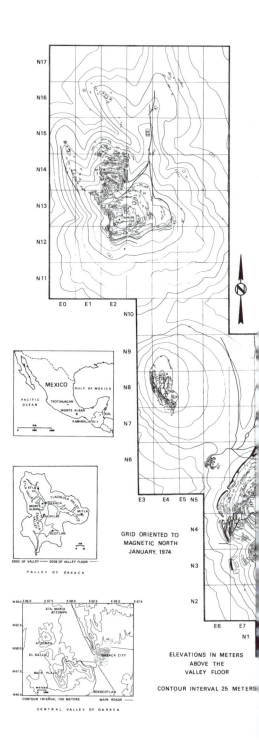

2.2 Monte Albán, showing
surface archaeological
remains dating to Monte
Albán Period IIIB (A.D.
500–700).

MONTE ALBAN

OAXACA, MEXICO

CHAEOLOGICAL AND TOPOGRAPHIC MAP

KEY	LEGEND
NORTH PLATFORM	RESIDENTIAL TERRACES _ _ _ _ _
SOUTH PLATFORM	MOUNDED BUILDINGS _ _ _ _ _
BUILDING OF THE DANZANTES	EXCAVATED BUILDINGS _ _ _ _
SIETE VENADO SYSTEM	STONE WALLS _ _ _ _ _ _ _ _
TOMB 7	DEFENSIVE WALLS _ _ _ _ _
EL GALLO	ANCIENT ROADS _ _ _ _ _ _ _
ATZOMPA	MODERN PAVED ROADS _ _ _ _
TOMB 104	

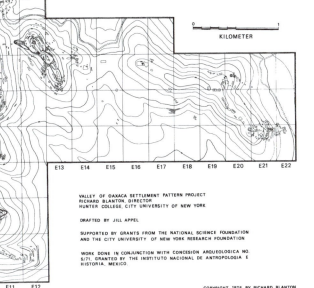

MAP SHOWS MAXIMUM EXTENT OF THE SITE CA. A.D. 600.
INTERPRETATIONS OF BUILDINGS IN THE MAIN PLAZA AREA ARE BASED
ON PLANS PUBLISHED BY THE INSTITUTO NACIONAL DE ANTROPOLOGIA E
HISTORIA, MEXICO, AND INTERPRETATIONS MADE BY MEMBERS OF THE
VALLEY OF OAXACA SETTLEMENT PATTERN PROJECT. ALL OTHER
INTERPRETATIONS ARE BASED ON SURFACE REMAINS MAPPED BY
MEMBERS OF THE VALLEY OF OAXACA SETTLEMENT PATTERN PROJECT.

0 KILOMETER 1

VALLEY OF OAXACA SETTLEMENT PATTERN PROJECT
RICHARD BLANTON, DIRECTOR
HUNTER COLLEGE, CITY UNIVERSITY OF NEW YORK

DRAFTED BY JILL APPEL

SUPPORTED BY GRANTS FROM THE NATIONAL SCIENCE FOUNDATION
AND THE CITY UNIVERSITY OF NEW YORK RESEARCH FOUNDATION

WORK DONE IN CONJUNCTION WITH CONCESION ARQUEOLOGICA NO.
5/71, GRANTED BY THE INSTITUTO NACIONAL DE ANTROPOLOGIA E
HISTORIA, MEXICO.

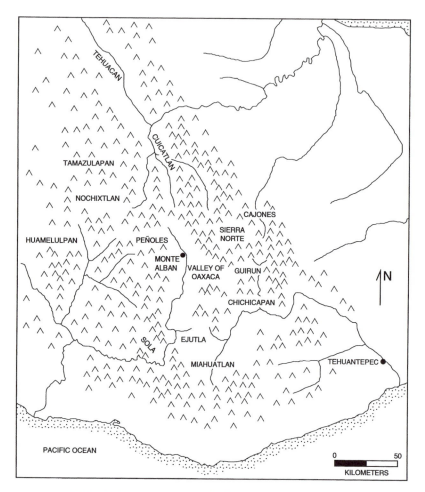

2.3 The Valley of Oaxaca and adjacent regions in the southern highlands.

the technologies that were available to past Oaxacan farmers. It is important to remember that pre-Hispanic farmers in Oaxaca relied principally on stone axes, hoes, and wooden digging sticks. Having no large draft animals (such as cattle, horses, mules, oxen, or water buffalo) or wheeled vehicles, they did not employ the plow. Archaeological finds and botanical analyses have shown us that the size of maize cobs and therefore the productivity of this staple crop increased during the pre-Hispanic era.

Through careful excavation procedures such as the screening of archaeological sediments through fine mesh and flotation to recover plant

Box 4 *Mixtec, Zapotec, Mixe: the question of identity*

Who were the inhabitants of the Valley of Oaxaca at 1500 B.C. and 500 B.C.? Who were the builders of Monte Albán? What is the name of this civilization? Archaeologists have relatively little interest in such questions; naming groups of people of course has no effect on what the people responsible for the archaeological record did in the past, and their presumed identity should have no influence on archaeologists' analysis and interpretation. It is more important for us to know that cultural groups were being formed and why than to give them names. One cultural boundary in Oaxaca that is relatively easy to recognize today (though not the most important in terms of social or political action) is linguistic. Most people in Oaxaca speak Spanish, but according to the national census about 45 percent of the state's population of 2.5 million also speak one of the sixteen (or sixty, counting the many dialects) indigenous languages.

The main native languages in and around the Valley of Oaxaca today are Mixe, in the mountains to the east of the valley; Mixtec, in the mountains to the west of the valley and historically, at least since late pre-Hispanic times, in many places in the western valley itself; and Zapotec, in the Valley of Oaxaca and in the mountains to the north and south. Monte Albán has usually been considered an ancient city of Zapotec speakers, and its now-extinct writing is a form of Zapotec. What roles non-Zapotec speakers, including Mixe and Mixtec, played at Monte Albán and in its regional state are not known.

remains, archaeologists have obtained evidence of ancient food consumption. These studies of subsistence debris have been supplemented by human skeletal research that also can yield insights into past diet and health. Chemical analysis of samples of human bone from Monte Albán by Jennifer A. Blitz (1995) has shed light on ancient subsistence, and a skeletal analysis of Monte Albán burials by Denise C. Hodges (1989) has reconstructed pre-Hispanic patterns of health and disease.

Our discussions center on the Valley of Oaxaca and its immediate surroundings, but we also draw on research from more distant locales. Most important are surveys and excavations by Charles S. Spencer and Elsa Redmond in the Cuicatlán Cañada, a long, narrow river canyon situated between the Valley of Oaxaca and the Tehuacán Valley (Redmond 1983; Spencer 1982; Spencer and Redmond 1997). The floor of the tropical Cañada averages 500–700 meters in elevation, well below the temperate Valley of Oaxaca (at 1,500 meters). The people in the Cañada could grow tropical fruits unavailable at higher elevations. Excavations and surveys also have been carried out in the Mixteca Alta, a region of mountains and intermontane valleys (e.g., Balkansky 1998; Byland 1980; Byland and Pohl 1994; Spores 1972; Zárate 1987). We draw on findings from projects conducted along the Pacific Coast of Oaxaca by Robert and Judith Zeitlin (J. Zeitlin 1978; R. Zeitlin 1978, 1993), Arthur Joyce (1993), and Donald Brockington (1957).

Our holistic approach (see also Blanton, Kowalewski, Feinman, and

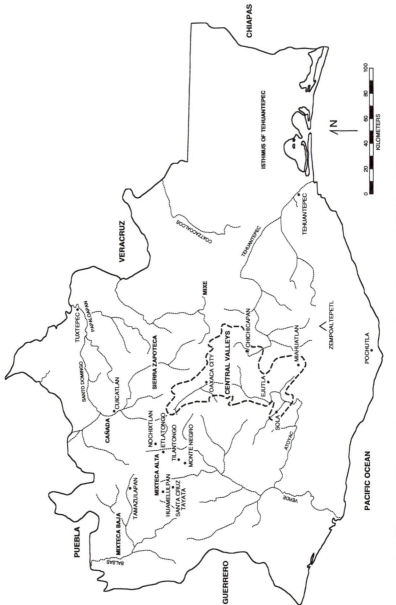

2.4 The state of Oaxaca, showing sites and regions adjacent to the Valley of Oaxaca.

Finsten 1993) to the rise of the state requires this multiscalar (household, community, region, macroregion) and multidisciplinary (e.g., archaeology, epigraphy, geography, skeletal analysis) perspective. Our analytical considerations range from political economy to ancient land use to iconographic analysis. Admittedly, this study can be complicated – but cultural systems are themselves complicated, especially when viewed over centuries.

The physical environment

The Valley of Oaxaca is the largest expanse of flat land (roughly 2,500 square kilometers) in Mexico's rugged southern highlands (fig. 2.5). The valley is the upper drainage basin of the Atoyac River and its tributary, the Río Salado. Smaller valleys – Ejutla, Sola, Miahuatlán, and Chichicapan – abut or lie near the valley on the south. These valleys have an average elevation of 1,500 meters and are ringed by mountains that rise to 3,000 meters above sea level. Most of the remainder of the state of Oaxaca also is composed of rugged mountains; the highest point is the dormant volcano Zempoaltepetl (southeast of Miahuatlán), at 3,750 meters above sea level.

We discuss land and water here because these are the resources that the Valley of Oaxaca has in abundance relative to the surrounding regions. The neighboring valleys have narrower floodplains and less farmland than the Valley of Oaxaca. They are higher and colder (Chichicapan), drier (Ejutla and Miahuatlán), or much smaller (Sola).

The terrain of the Valley of Oaxaca is divided into three basic topographic zones – alluvium, piedmont, and mountains – that provide diverse resources and varied farming opportunities (Kirkby 1973; Nicholas 1989) (fig. 2.6). The alluvium or floodplain, which abuts the Atoyac River and its tributaries, is the valley's flattest terrain and has the thickest, richest soils. In many parts of the alluvial zone, shallow wells easily can be dug to the water table, providing the opportunity for well irrigation even in dry years. For millennia the occupants of the valley have dug 1 to 5-meter-deep wells into which they lower pots to retrieve the water. The full pots are then used to hand-carry the water directly to the plants. The fertile soils, relatively gentle grades, and opportunities for irrigation make the alluvium the most favorable farmland in the valley. Originally, the alluvium was heavily forested, but once settled by farming peoples it rapidly became a highly desirable setting for agriculture and was almost totally cleared. The loss of valley-floor forest was probably one of the environmental consequences of the rise of the state.

Above the alluvium lies the foothills or piedmont zone. Compared to

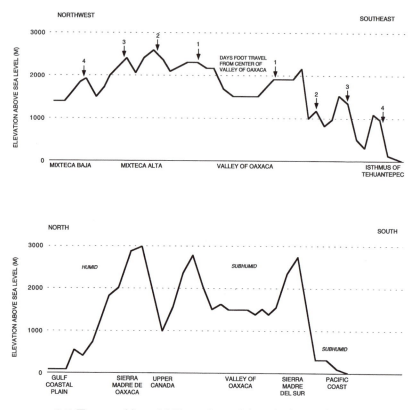

2.5 Topographic variability and travel times in the southern highlands.

the alluvium, the piedmont has thinner soils and more pronounced slopes. Because the water table is much deeper here, the natural vegetation (as well as agricultural activity) is more heavily dependent on rainfall. For this reason, the natural vegetal cover is typically thinner, and agrarian production is more risky than in the alluvium. Yet, in a wet year, high maize yields can be produced in many sections of the piedmont.

The piedmont grades up to more mountainous terrain. Surrounding the valley, the mountains of Oaxaca are still covered with dense stands of oak and pine. The mountains generally provide fewer opportunities for reliable farming than the alluvium and the piedmont, but these forested uplands were the principal source of timber and deer.

The key determinant of agricultural yield in the valley is the availability of water (Kirkby 1973). The Valley of Oaxaca is semiarid, with a valley-wide average of 550 millimeters (22 inches) of annual rainfall. Precipitation occurs primarily during the May-to-October wet season,

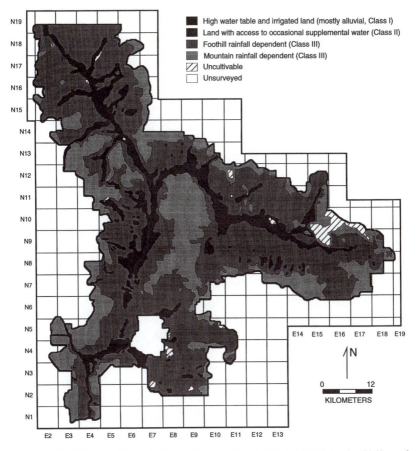

2.6 Distribution of three classes of agricultural land in the Valley of Oaxaca.

turning a brown-gray-yellow dry season (November to April) environment into a verdant green landscape. Rainfall is highly variable spatially,
seasonally, and from year to year. In an average year, a given locale
receives between 400 and 800 millimeters of rain. If propitiously timed,
this is marginally adequate to produce a single crop of maize.
Supplemental water from wells, small-scale canal irrigation, and
floodwater runoff helps prevent crop failures in many years; in some parts
of the valley it may support more than one crop per year.

The Valley of Oaxaca is markedly different from the mountainous
terrain that surrounds it for approximately 200 kilometers in every direction. Yet this great breadth of flat land also is internally diverse. The valley

is shaped like a Y with the right arm bent down. The northern or Etla arm is narrow and fairly dry but offers the best opportunities for irrigation. To the south lies the largest segment of the valley, the Valle Grande. Typically, it receives somewhat more rain than other areas of the valley, so dry (rainfall) farming is more productive. The Valle Grande also has more land that can be farmed by irrigation, drainage works, or tapping the high water table. But because of its greater size, a smaller proportion of its arable land is irrigable than in Etla. The eastern, Tlacolula arm has less irrigation potential and also receives less rain in most years. Farming generally is a riskier endeavor in Tlacolula.

Where the three arms of the Valley of Oaxaca converge is a knot of low hills that rise above the valley floor; it was on these hills that the urban center of Monte Albán was situated. We often refer to this section of the valley, within a 10-kilometer radius of the ancient capital, as the "central" area. Generally, the land here does not have high agricultural potential (Nicholas 1989). This area also was most influenced by the ancient capital.

The temperate Valley of Oaxaca lacked many of the goods that were highly prized by pre-Hispanic people, such as cacao, brightly colored bird feathers, marine shell, jade, turquoise, and tropical fruits. Most cotton had to be imported from the lowlands, where growing conditions were more suitable for it. Obsidian, a volcanic glass that is more easily worked and produces a sharper cutting edge than the locally available chert and quartz, also had to be procured from distant locales. The Valley of Oaxaca's relative poverty in these other key resources reinforced the significance of its potential to produce a wealth of food.

Before Monte Albán

The San José phase

Human occupation of the Valley of Oaxaca goes back some 10,000 years, but people began living in sedentary villages, growing crops as a main subsistence pursuit, and making pottery around 2000–1500 B.C. We begin our discussion of human activity in the valley at about 1000 B.C., in the middle of the Early Formative San José phase. This was the time of the Early Horizon "Olmec" art, discussed previously, and a key turning point in the evolution of social complexity in the Valley of Oaxaca, as it was elsewhere in Mesoamerica. But was the Early Horizon, with its pan-Mesoamerican "Olmec" style and symbolic themes, a necessary evolutionary step in the direction of the later development of Mesoamerican civilization (e.g., Grove 1997)? We return to consider the evolutionary significance of the "Olmec" phenomenon in our concluding chapter. The scale of society in the Valley of Oaxaca was small during the San José phase, and it did not change appreciably until Period I, when the early state evolved (Kowalewski et al. 1989:ch. 3). We estimate a total population of about 2,000 for the region at 1000 B.C., far below what anthropologists associate with the minimum population sizes for most early states. Such low numbers are in the size range of many well-described Native American societies of historic times (e.g., the Pueblo societies of the American Southwest, the small chiefdoms of the Northwest Coast, and the tribal subdivisions of the Huron and Iroquois).

In contrast with some of these small-scale societies, the population of the Valley of Oaxaca evidenced some social inequality among households by the San José phase, although not to the degree seen during the first millennium A.D. and later. The indications of social inequality at 1000 B.C. come from excavated houses, burials, and other features (Flannery and Marcus 1994; Marcus and Flannery 1996:ch. 8; see also Feinman et al. 1985; Kowalewski et al. 1989:ch. 3 for additional data from regional surveys).

The study of burials nearly always proves invaluable for an archaeologist attempting to understand social inequality, and this is true in Oaxaca. During the San José phase, high-status burials, so identified by the presence of fancier than usual grave goods such as decorated ceramic vessels, magnetite mirrors, and elaborate jade pieces, were found tightly flexed. This positioning probably reflects some special treatment, involving wrapping, that bodies received prior to burial. Lower-status individuals, interred with fewer and plainer grave goods, generally were buried in extended positions. The graves of higher-ranking individuals also tended to be covered by stone slabs. These individuals were more likely to be buried with multiple wives or retainers and to have deformed skulls. Skull deformation was a sign of beauty and high status among some Mesoamerican peoples and was practiced on certain infants by binding the head shortly after birth. Such depictions are seen in pictoral sources from later periods, and we assume this practice was an indicator of high status during the San José phase as well.

Body posture may be another indicator of status differences. Certain ceramic figurines display what Marcus and Flannery interpret as obeisance postures, that is, postures that show deference to persons of high status. The artifact assemblages found in houses indicate considerable variation in degree of household access to major prestige goods, including mica, marine shell, jade, magnetite, and decorated pottery, some of which were imported from distant regions outside the valley. The houses themselves varied in quality; for example, finer houses have whitewashed walls.

Wattle and daub (wooden posts, sticks, and mud plaster) was the major construction method, and size differences between houses were not great, although one excavated structure at the site of Tomaltepec, which may have been a house, was built on a meter-high platform (Whalen 1981:38–43). We can infer from excavated data recovered through screening and flotation that some households apparently ate more venison than others. Overall, the various material indicators point in the direction of differences in wealth and status between households but do not provide evidence of sharply distinct social classes.

Inequality also is seen in the differential growth of one community. San José Mogote, in the Etla arm of the valley, grew to some 1,000 persons, approximately ten times the size of the next largest community. Evidently, some combination of economic, ritual, and political activities had been concentrated primarily in this settlement, attracting households who migrated there to live (growth may have been due as well to the higher fertility of the community's families). Compared with other areas of the valley, San José Mogote also has more evidence for the specialized production and the import and export of prestige goods.

Wealth, prestige, status, and power

One of the most challenging aspects of any anthropological analysis is to understand the relationships among wealth (control of material resources), prestige (esteem), status (social position), and power (the ability of one person or group to direct the actions of others). The power dimension of inequality has received the most attention in anthropological research on state formation and its antecedents (e.g., Service 1971:140 and passim). How is it that power comes to be concentrated in the hands of certain groups or persons? Although some differences in power are found in all human societies (for example, within households, based on gender and generation), in a category of societies that we call chiefdoms positions of power relevant to governance somehow come to be limited so that not all those persons with sufficient talent to occupy such statuses actually achieve them (here we paraphrase Morton Fried [1967:109]). In anthropological theories of state formation (e.g., Service 1975:15–16), chiefdoms are considered a stage of political evolution antecedent and transitional to states. Obviously, then, we want to know when and how chiefdoms evolved in the Valley of Oaxaca.

It is evident that wealth differences existed in the valley in 1000 B.C. and that control of wealth was tied in part to differential access to foreign, exotic goods. Some households were linked into social networks extending to other Mesoamerican regions where these goods originated. The members of these households were treated differentially in life and in death; they had relatively high prestige and perhaps special social positions or statuses. Did these same households also have power in society? No known household controlled the bulk of specialized production or exchange of exotic goods, although the number of households involved in such exchange constitutes a small minority. Nor did any particular household or group monopolize access to important supernatural forces. In fact, two distinct symbolic sets (described below) predominated in religious imagery, and neither of these was monopolized by a particular household, neighborhood, or community.

Although chiefly households known ethnographically and historically often reside in especially elaborate houses (e.g., Helms 1979:9), in the Valley of Oaxaca of 1000 B.C. no elite residence is known that would be analogous to, for example, the elevated chiefs' houses of southeastern North American chiefdoms such as the Natchez (Nabokov 1989:96–97). By the second half of the San José phase, the major architectural feature of San José Mogote was an 18-meter-wide stone-faced terrace upon which sat a multitiered pyramidal platform some 2 meters high (Marcus and Flannery 1996:108–10). Access to the broad terrace surface in front of the platform was by way of two narrow staircases. Two carved stones, bearing feline and bird imagery, had been incorporated into an extension of the terrace face, strongly suggesting that the terraced space was symbolically important. Some of the stones used in the construction of the terrace-facing wall had been brought in from other places in the Etla Valley, perhaps signifying the participation of other communities in the construction and use of the ceremonial space (Marcus and Flannery 1996:110). There is no house architecturally connected to or located on the platform, suggesting that the complex was a public, nonresidential ceremonial space rather than a chiefly residence. In sum, no architectural feature, whether house, burial mound, or any other, can be said to glorify or commemorate any particular group, household, or individual.

In the absence of any secure architectural indicators, evidence of the existence of a chieftainship might be found in the kinship organization of society. In many ethnographically and historically known chiefdoms, in Polynesia and sub-Saharan Africa and elsewhere, political power is vested in a hierarchy of officeholders centered on one household and its chiefly head. Often, this person is the highest-ranking member of the highest-ranking descent group (Service 1971:ch. 5; 1975: ch. 4). In these cases, the society as a whole (or, at least, its most prominent households) is organized as a system of kin groups made up of persons who trace their descent through either males or females (i.e., unilineally) to a common ancestor. In some chiefdoms, certain descent groups establish their political and social preeminence and their control of wealth on the basis of a reckoning of descent that links high-ranking individuals through many generations of distinguished ancestors to the society's founders or to powerful supernatural forces. Secondary elites depend for their status on their genealogical nearness to the chief. Anthropologists refer to these various arrangements as systems of ranked descent groups, conical clan systems, ramages, or ranked society.

There may be evidence of descent reckoning in the Valley of Oaxaca of 1000 B.C. At San José Mogote and several other excavated communities, carved pottery depicts two distinct symbolic patterns, one stylistically representing lightning or sky (the fire-serpent) and the other earth (portrayed as "earthquake") (Flannery and Marcus 1994:136–39; Marcus 1989). That this pottery may refer to male descent groups is indicated by the fact that only males (including children) are buried with the carved imagery. Further, these decorated pots symbolize spatially distinct social groupings. Some whole communities are associated with either sky or earth; at San José Mogote the community was partitioned into two areas, one sky and the other earth (Pyne 1976). In addition, as Marcus and Flannery (1996:105) remind us, children's burials in some cases include high-status items, and this may indicate that status was conferred by descent-group membership (ascribed) rather than achieved.

Although many anthropologists correctly link the emergence of chiefdoms to the hereditary ranking of descent groups, we doubt that hereditary ranking or a chiefdom (in Service's sense) was present in the Valley of Oaxaca at 1000 B.C. Because a funeral may reflect the status of a deceased person's household as much as that of the person himself or herself (see, e.g., Cannon 1989), we cannot assume that an elaborate child's burial reflects ascribed status. Another discrepancy that we see in the data of 1000 B.C. relates to the nature of craft production and other economic activities of households at San José Mogote. In many chiefdoms known ethnographically elite households frequently are exempt from any direct involvement in production, depending instead on tribute from other households and their control of the labor of craft specialists (e.g., Earle 1987; Helms 1979:14, 15). At San José Mogote, however, high-status households were involved in the normal range of subsistence activities. Their storage pits and food preparation facilities and implements are similar to those of lower-ranking households, and they may in fact have processed exotic goods more than their lower-ranked contemporaries. For example, an elite house excavated by Flannery and Marcus (1994:333–39) contains evidence for cooking, food storage, the smoothing of wood, the manufacture of heat-treated chert bifaces, basket making, pearl oyster ornament manufacture, and pottery making. This was hardly a household exempt from work or one whose status was clearly determined through descent reckoning. What it suggests is that wealth and status accrued to households that were central to exchange networks linking them to people in other regions and that turned out goods involved in these exchanges in large quantities.

Ethnographic examples of systems that link prestige and wealth to exchange and production rather than to descent reckoning include certain "big-man" societies of Highland New Guinea (such as the Kapauku [Pospisil 1963:214–15]) and the seventeenth-through nineteenth-century Plains Indians (e.g., Lewis 1942). In both of these cases, influential household heads were successful in part because they were able to assemble and motivate a household capable of high levels of production (for example, on the Plains, in fur processing). One of the strategies they employed to this end was expanding the working capacity of the household through polygyny (Lewis 1942). The association of high-status individuals with multiple burials in the Valley of Oaxaca suggests that this may have been one strategy for building a productive household during the San José phase as well.

Moiety organization rather than a chiefdom?

How do people manage to incorporate competing "big men" and their factions into a single, integrated society? On the Plains of western North America, the creative solutions developed to solve this problem included elaborate tribal rituals, tribal councils, rotating chiefships, medicine and war societies, and many other mechanisms of social integration (e.g., Hoebel 1978). For us, the most pervasive feature of social structure of the San José phase of the Valley of Oaxaca is not a system of ranked descent groups but the duality of earth-and-sky symbolism. We suggest that this dual emphasis is inconsistent with social structure based on unilineal descent. Unilineal descent-group systems such as those of the Hopi, the Northwest Coast Indians, the Iroquois, and the Huron are much more fragmented (Driver 1969:248, map 33), although some cases also have a dual grouping of descent groups (moieties). Typically the society is made up of more than two descent groups, each with its own totemic symbolism, sacred objects, emblems, residences or clusters of houses, rituals, and even ritual structures. For example, the Hopi, with a turn-of-the-twentieth-century population of about 2,000 (the same as the Valley of Oaxaca in 1000 B.C.), were divided into about thirty clans (Ortiz 1979; Titiev 1944). Some grouping of related clans (called phratries) occurred, but even combined in this way there were fourteen groupings rather than just two.

Social structure based on descent groups is likely to show greater diversity in symbolism than we have in the Valley of Oaxaca at 1000 B.C. Given the wide distribution of earth-and-sky symbolism throughout Mesoamerica during the Early Horizon (Coe 1989; Flannery and Marcus 1994:387), it is difficult to see how it could have represented the same descent groups over such a large, culturally diverse area. This degree of uniformity seems unlikely since descent group systems in general tend to be variable from region to region. This discrepancy throws additional doubt on the hypothesis that the Valley of Oaxaca had a political structure based on descent reckoning.

A significant feature of the valley's symbolic system of 1000 B.C. is its emphasis on two primary principles, sky and earth, manifested as lightning and earthquake. Together they represented the most important supernatural forces affecting humans. But they are, at the same time, opposites, reflecting the contrastive nature of supernatural power. This brings to mind other instances of dual symbolic systems that are thought to contribute to the integration of social systems. The anthropologist A. R. Radcliffe-Brown referred to this process as "opposition." As Radcliffe-Brown (quoted in Kuper 1977:65–66) expressed it, the

Yin-Yang philosophy of ancient China is the systematic elaboration of the principle that can be used to define the social structure of moieties in Australian tribes, for the structure of moieties is . . . one of a unity of opposing groups, in the double sense that the two groups are friendly opponents, and they are represented as being in some sense opposites, in the way in which eaglehawk and crow or black and white are opposites.

Eggan (1950:302) writes in a similar vein about the dual organization of New Mexico Pueblos such as the Tewa: "dual organizations in a broad sense are devices to organize and regulate rivalry and opposition in order to serve the purposes of the group as a whole. . . Ceremonial dual divisions . . . reflect differences in seasonal activities, observations of solar phenomena, and the like; they control ceremonial rivalry by regulating competition and dividing responsibility in channeled areas" (cf. Lowell 1996).

We lack the data that would allow us to understand the dual divisions in the Valley of Oaxaca of 1000 B.C. in detail, but the pervasive duality of earth-and-sky symbolism suggests that social integration was achieved through a principle of moiety opposition rather than through the centralized political offices of a chieftainship. A productive analogy for San José Mogote and the rest of the Valley of Oaxaca in 1000 B.C. might be found among ethnographically described Mesoamerican peasant communities with moiety structures. This pattern of dualistically partitioned communities (which in some cases links outlying dependent communities to partitions of a central one) is regarded by cultural anthropologists as a survival of an ancient aboriginal Mesoamerican social structure, because most of the communities still displaying it are those that were least influenced by Spanish imperial policies. In addition, there are no known Spanish or more recent Mexican government policies that would have produced it (Hunt and Nash 1967:261–68).

These dual partitions or barrios generally are not composed of ranked unilineal descent groups such as the conical clan systems of chiefdoms (Beals 1945; Hunt and Nash 1967:261–68). Indeed, Mesoamerica is not recognized as an area in which unilineal descent played an important role in aboriginal social structure (Driver 1969:map 32). Furthermore, moiety structure and descent groups need not coexist; many known moiety systems (for example, the Tewa Pueblos of New Mexico) exist in the absence of descent group structure (Beals 1945).

The dual partitions or barrios known ethnographically have primarily ceremonial and political functions. For example, among the Western Mixe speakers of the mountains just north and east of the Valley of Oaxaca (Beals 1945), each barrio has its own saint as a key symbol and is charged with carrying out the associated saint's-day ritual. In addition to ritual, governance of Mixe communities is structured by the dual system. An important feature of dual governance is that it prevents the concentration of power in any one group or household. At any one time the two most important Mixe officials, mayor and judge, must be of different barrios, and these offices are reversed between barrios annually. Lower officials involved in day-to-day governance rotate offices between barrios in alternate weeks.

Applying a dual-barrio analogy to the Valley of Oaxaca of 1000 B.C. does not provide all the answers about how society was governed, but it does allow us to posit a political structure in which governance was corporate – in which power was shared across the main constituent groups of society rather than being vested primarily in a specific chiefly household or high-ranking descent group. Given the social and wealth inequality apparent in the San José phase, it is interesting that in some ethnographically known Native American societies, such as the Plains tribes mentioned above, various systems of corporate governance permitted considerable leeway for individual households to engage in trade and to accumulate prestige and even wealth (Hoebel 1978). At the same time, these systems of governance prevented the concentration of power in the hands of particular wealthy or prestigious families or groups (see, e.g., Trigger 1990). Interestingly in light of our Oaxaca case, these Native American systems often reflect the application of concepts of dual governance, for example, in the distinction frequently made between peace (or internal) chief and war (or external) chief (e.g., Miller 1955).

We conclude that in the Valley of Oaxaca of 1000 B.C. it was possible for some households to accumulate wealth and prestige to a degree not seen previously. The major cause of the growing social differentiation was participation in the Early Horizon interaction sphere. Especially at San José Mogote, important households with ties to distant regions were able to obtain exotic goods that served as personal adornments, were used in ritual, and were buried with esteemed individuals. We do not doubt that these same well-connected households played important political roles in society, although how power was exercised and who exercised it are still unclear. Although participation in the Mesoamerican interaction sphere by Valley of Oaxaca households was a cause for the growing differences in access to wealth and prestige, it did not produce a centralized chiefdom of the type anthropologists consider a stepping-stone to the state. Instead, the Valley of Oaxaca combined a dual symbolic system with community-based ritual, and this was built around a dual social structure of barrios and their dependent communities. This was a corporate local government embedded in a larger, Mesoamerican social network.

The Middle Formative

By the Middle Formative Rosario phase (700–500 B.C.) the Early Horizon interaction sphere had changed substantially (Grove 1987). While some goods, such as obsidian, continued to be exchanged over long distances, by the end of this phase the amount of intergroup interaction and stylistic sharing had declined. For example, many localized ceramic styles had developed in different Mesoamerican regions (e.g., Demarest 1989). In the Valley of Oaxaca, some fancy pottery of the Rosario phase still expressed symbolic themes that were seen in the San José phase, especially earth symbolism, but other decoration appears to consist of geometric designs that may have had less specific symbolic content. The system of dual barrios did not continue through the Middle Formative, and at this point we do not fully understand what kind of social system had developed to replace it (see Feinman et al. 1985; Kowalewski et al. 1989:ch. 4; Marcus and Flannery 1996:ch. 10).

During the Rosario phase, San José Mogote continued as the region's major center, but other communities had grown substantially. Huitzo in the far northern end of the Etla arm, Tilcajete in the Valle Grande, and Yegüih in the Tlacolula arm are the most important such "head towns" (fig. 2.7). Surrounding these centers were clusters of smaller communities. These site clusters, consisting of centers plus dependent communities, were separated from each other by largely unoccupied areas that we interpret as buffer zones (contested areas in which settlement would have

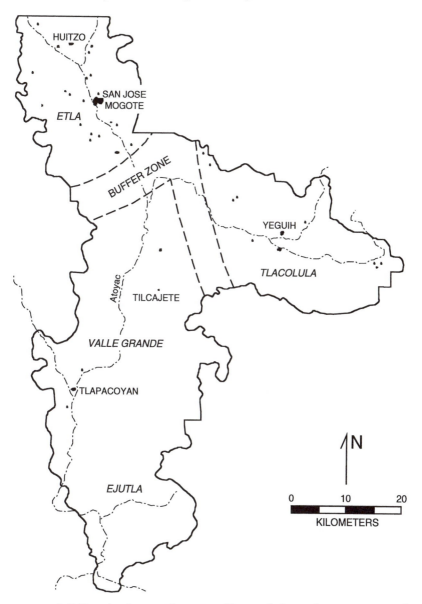

2.7 Rosario-phase settlements with populations of ten or more and buffer zones.

been unsafe). These changes in settlement pattern suggest the development of competing polities and a reduction of San José Mogote regional dominance.

There was evidently a considerable amount of public construction in the various head towns. At San José Mogote, Flannery and Marcus excavated a large Rosario-phase platform (Structure 19) atop a high hill. The culmination of several building stages here was a platform roughly 22 by 29 meters supported by large quarried limestone blocks, some weighing half a ton. The platform's west-facing staircase led to a lime-plastered platform (Structure 28) on which stood a large wattle-and-daub temple. Thus, an Early Formative social system that devoted more energy to the construction of public ritual buildings than to the construction of elite residences or burial monuments of chiefs persisted but on a grander scale. (Later in the Rosario phase, however, this temple and its platform were superseded by an elite residence.)

Excavations in and around Structure 19 provide intriguing evidence of an important element of the changing social system of the later Rosario phase. At some point the temple atop Structure 28 had been intentionally burned, suggesting conflict between communities or within San José Mogote itself. In a passageway between Structure 19 and another large Rosario-phase platform, Flannery and Marcus discovered an impressive carved-stone monument (Monument 3) that is the first of its kind (fig. 2.8). On this slab was carved a naked man, whose heart had been removed. This figure, its accompanying hieroglyphs (indicating that his name may have been "1 Earthquake"), and other evidence from the Structure 19 area led Marcus and Flannery (1996:130) to several inferences about the Rosario phase:

(1) The 260–day calendar clearly existed by this time. (2) The use of Xòo, a known Zapotec day-name, relates the hieroglyphs to an archaic form of the Zapotec language. (3) The carving makes clear that Rosario phase sacrifice was not limited to drawing one's own blood with stingray spines; it now included human sacrifice by heart removal. (4) Since 1 Earthquake is shown naked, even stripped of whatever ornaments he might have worn, he fits our sixteenth-century descriptions of prisoners taken in battle. This carving of a prisoner, combined with the burning of the temple on Structure 28, suggests that by 600 B.C. the well-known Zapotec pattern of raiding, temple-burning, and capture of enemies for sacrifice had begun. (5) Many later Mesoamerican peoples, including the Maya, set carvings of their defeated enemies where they could be literally and metaphorically "trod upon." The horizontal placement of Monument 3 suggests that it, too, was designed for that visual metaphor.

Sometime after Structure 28 was burned, still within the Rosario phase, this same location, commanding a hill 15 meters above the rest of

2.8 Top and side views of Monument 3 at San José Mogote, discovered by Joyce Marcus and Kent V. Flannery. Drawing by Mark Orsen, courtesy of Joyce Marcus. Length 1.45 m.

the settlement, was used for the construction of an elaborate residence. The site chosen for this commanding house, one previously used for communal ritual, suggests increasing concentration of power in the hands of a particular household or households rather than in social-integrative rituals and their public ceremonial spaces.

In previous phases, all houses, regardless of status, were built near the center of an open yard. The Rosario-phase elite house described here took the form of an interior patio surrounded by room complexes (Marcus and Flannery 1996: fig. 139), much like the later houses in the valley, whose floor plans tended to restrict access to the more private living spaces of a patio and adjacent rooms that faced onto it. Its construction was of adobe rather than the usual wattle and daub, indicating a growing dichotomy in the material worlds of elite and nonelite. Although the house produced little evidence of craft production, its members may have been oriented toward military activities (suggested by an offering of eleven obsidian projectile points) and ritual (suggested by whistles and bloodletting tools).

Additionally, this household may have made use of descent rhetoric in a manner not seen previously. An anthropomorphic brazier found here could be a predecessor of incense burners that later figured in Zapotec rituals of ancestor worship (Marcus and Flannery 1996: fig. 141). A large (2-by-3 meter) stone-lined, two-chambered tomb under the house's patio is also the earliest known example of a major feature of Zapotec elite houses. Like the brazier, the tomb likely signifies an intensifying interest in connecting the household to its forebears through the material culture of ancestor worship. The brazier and tomb still do not constitute definitive evidence of a system of ranked descent groups, but they do suggest that by the Rosario phase there may have been more use of a rhetoric that claimed a connection between wealth, status, power, and ancestors. The use of the term "chiefdom" might be appropriate for this social formation, with the proviso that we still cannot be sure that ranked descent groups were part of the social matrix.

The next major step toward the development of the state in the Valley of Oaxaca was the founding of a new regional political capital at Monte Albán. The Rosario-phase social context for this profound transformation included increased political fragmentation in the region, the development of a warfare-sacrifice complex, and an evident increase in the degree of political centralization. An additional set of factors conditioning the choice to build a new capital was the changing nature of the Mesoamerican world of the latter Middle Formative period. By 500 B.C. the Mesoamerican interaction sphere of the Early Horizon had largely disintegrated and regionalism had increased. Many of the communities that had played major roles in the interaction sphere – Tlatilco in the Basin of Mexico, San Lorenzo in Veracruz, and Chalcatzingo in Morelos – were no longer active, or had diminished roles; in their stead new centers had emerged. In this changing social environment, it may have been difficult for people to maintain the social ties that supplied exotic goods, and this too could have brought increased uncertainty and conflict. A dynamic, perhaps chaotic or unpredictable Mesoamerican scene may have been another factor conditioning the decision to establish a new form of political structure, one that had the capacity to integrate the Valley of Oaxaca into a single political system.

3 The origins of Monte Albán

Just after 500 B.C. pottery makers in the Valley of Oaxaca modified many of the ceramic types they had fashioned during what we call the Rosario phase and began making a number of distinctive kinds of pottery vessels (box 5). This ceramic change permits today's archaeologists to identify and distinguish sites of the ceramic phase that follows Rosario, Monte Albán Early I (500–300 B.C.) – the first phase of a period that extended to 100 B.C. A period called "I" occurs so late in the valley's ceramic sequence, nearly one thousand years later than the appearance of the earliest pottery, because the first stratigraphic excavations in the valley were conducted at Monte Albán, a site whose history commenced around 500 B.C. The pottery found in the lowest stratigraphic levels (Period I) was assumed to be the earliest in the valley. As illustrated in the previous chapter, subsequent research at more ancient sites such as San José Mogote found several pre-Monte Albán phases, but we still use the terminology of the Monte Albán ceramic sequence.

The social and cultural changes that began during Early I and continued into Late I were epochal ones in the valley's history; they are felt in many respects right up to the present day. Not all aspects of these changes can be described as thoroughly as we would like, because most of the Oaxacan archaeological record is still unexplored. Yet various lines of archaeological and epigraphic evidence point to a profound transformation of society, technology, and culture. The most important change was the development of a more socially integrated valley society. For the first time in its roughly 1,000–year history of settled agricultural life, the valley's social system was strongly organized around a single dominant community that was clearly a regional political capital. The establishment of the capital is the most prominent manifestation of a new political order in the Valley of Oaxaca. The new capital served as the focal point for cultural and political activities in the region from Early I (500 B.C.) until its collapse and virtual abandonment in roughly A.D. 700 (at the end of Period IIIB). What were the causes of this radical change in the organization of the regional system?

Box 5 *Pottery types, phases, periods, and archaeological sequences*

Archaeologists build time sequences using whatever techniques and materials will work in a particular region. Mesoamerican archaeologists use stratigraphy (finding earlier and overlying later levels in deposits laid down by nature or by ancient construction, as at Monte Albán), radiocarbon dates, changes in pottery styles, and even clues from the ancient Mesoamerican calendar, but the workhorse of dating is still the potsherd. Pottery does not deteriorate in the ground, and pre-Hispanic Mesoamericans made millions of pots in hundreds of styles. Alfonso Caso in the 1930s and archaeologists in Oaxaca ever since have been figuring out which specific pottery styles – types – were in vogue during which times in the past. Stratigraphic position provided the relative dates, and radiocarbon allowed some dates in years to be assigned. Some pottery styles, such as the were-jaguar designs of the Early Formative, are so distinctive and so widespread in Mesoamerica that once they are well dated in several known areas they can be used to help construct a ceramic sequence in regions that do not yet have good stratigraphy or radiocarbon dating. This use of types or styles from other regions is called cross-dating.

Once the popular pottery styles can be placed in chronological sequence and verified through one or more of the other dating methods, archaeologists can often tell at a glance when a site was occupied just from the pottery types found on the surface or in excavations. But in Oaxaca, this "when" is only approximate, usually within 200–300 years. The smallest units of archaeological time that we can recognize there, given current knowledge of the dating of pottery types, are phases: Tierras Largas, early and late San José, Guadalupe, Rosario, and Monte Albán Early I and Late I. Because pottery types vary from region to region, each region has its own set of type and phase names. Periods are the broader time spans, such as Early Formative and Monte Albán Period I. Periods exist in archaeological jargon because they were the time units archaeologists initially could recognize. Better knowledge of subtle style differences and further stratigraphic work often allows subdivision of periods into phases. Periods also are convenient for talking about what was happening during a particular time across many regions.

The new center

A marginal setting for a capital

Prior to Period I, only a few small villages dotted the landscape of the valley's central area. There was no occupation on Monte Albán itself. Few households had chosen the central area as a place to live before Early I, in part because it had been one of the valley's contested zones between Rosario-phase chiefdoms and may not have been a particularly safe place to live. More important, as we have seen, Monte Albán and its immediate hinterland are environmentally marginal for agricultural production by comparison with other parts of the valley. The site itself is a complex of high, rocky, eroded outcrops west of the major stream drainage, the Atoyac River (fig. 3.1, box 6). While the Atoyac was no doubt a source of water for the center's population, it is 4 kilometers from the highest point of the site, where the earliest settlement was concentrated. On the moun-

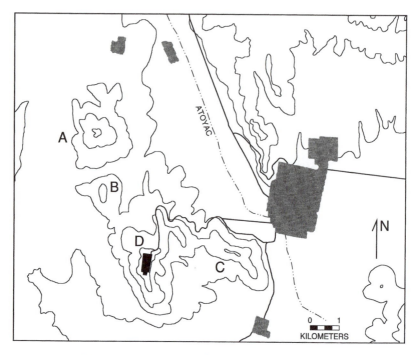

3.1 The physical setting of Monte Albán. Stippled areas are modern communities, including Oaxaca de Juárez, the state capital. Major sections of the ancient city are identified by letters; A=Cerro Atzompa, B=El Gallo, C=Monte Albán Chico, and D=the main ridge line of Monte Albán.

tain itself there are no naturally occurring sources of water. In later periods, several reservoirs were constructed within the community's boundaries that could have served as sources of drinking water (and, in one case, to supply a small irrigation system); however, during the city's earliest occupation, in Early I, almost all water would have been laboriously carried up the hill.

Additionally, it would not have been possible to grow the community's food supply either on the slopes of the rocky hill itself or in directly adjacent fields. Usually, a preindustrial community's agricultural catchment (i.e., main zone of agricultural production) would be a roughly circular area extending 2–4 kilometers from the site's edge. Studies of preindustrial agricultural villages have shown that this catchment radius is the maximum manageable distance from a community's dwellings to its agricultural fields (Chisholm 1968). Monte Albán's catchment zone and, indeed, the larger central area as a whole had only a limited potential for

Box 6 *The archaeological site of Monte Albán*

Monte Albán is the colonial-period name for the highest ridge of a complex of hills where the ancient Oaxacan capital was located. The site's aboriginal name is not known with certainty, but the hilltops that make up Monte Albán were given names in Mixtec and Nahuatl (the language of the Aztecs) on a colonial-era pictorial map. This map is kept by the town of Xoxocotlán, at the base of Monte Albán. On this map, the central hill shows a drum and a man in a bird helmet, and the words written next to it mean "hill of the lord" or "hill of the feathered head." The other prominent place-names are "hill of the jaguar" and "hill of the quetzal" (Caso, Bernal, and Acosta 1967:84; Marcus 1976:131; Smith 1973:202–10, figs. 162, 163).

During its period of maximum population size (Period IIIB, A.D. 500–700), Monte Albán extended over a complex of hills and ridges, including Cerro Atzompa, El Gallo, and Monte Albán Chico, as well as the main ridgeline of Monte Albán (fig. 3.1). At the highest point of this latter ridge, the valley's most massive complex of public buildings was constructed within and enclosing a plaza (the "Main Plaza") measuring some 250 by 100 meters.

Building a city on steep slopes was not easy. Flat space for houses and other constructions was created by leveling the sloping terrain and constructing stone-faced terraces. Although most houses and other buildings are no longer standing, terraces are still readily visible on the surface, and we used them as our basic units of data recording when we carried out the systematic surface survey of the site (Blanton 1978). We located, mapped, and surface collected approximately 2,000 terraces at Monte Albán and also recorded features such as reservoirs, canals, roads, and defensive walls. These survey data, combined with the architectural mapping and excavation projects carried out by Alfonso Caso, Ignacio Bernal, and others (e.g., Caso, Bernal, and Acosta 1967; Caso 1969), provide a rich data base for the study of the city's carved stone monuments, public architecture, population growth, neighborhoods, and craft-production industries, among many other topics.

agricultural production. Except for a few tiny patches of the most productive class of land, with deep, fertile soil and available water for irrigation (what we call Class I fields), and a small area of land with intermediate potential (Class II), this central portion of the Valley of Oaxaca contains primarily Class III land (i.e., land with the least potential for agricultural production) (Nicholas 1989). Production in the central area would not have been sufficient to feed the growing center's population (Nicholas 1989:493).

Even if all of Monte Albán's population had been engaged in farming (which we doubt could have been the case), the center could not have fed itself based on production in its catchment area alone. According to our calculations, Monte Albán's food must have been supplied by the surplus production of many villages in the central area and of communities in the Etla Valley and the adjacent northern part of the Valle Grande (fig. 3.2). Clearly, Monte Albán's "social catchment zone" (as distinct from its smaller, more immediate agricultural catchment zone) included an area

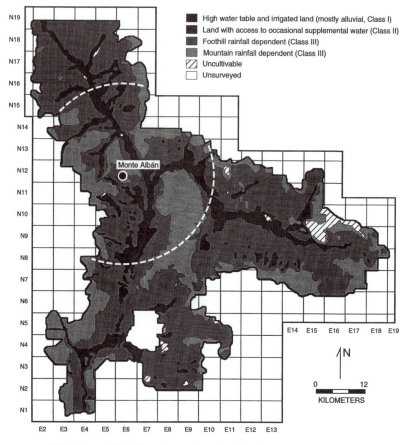

High water table and irrigated land (mostly alluvial, Class I)
Land with access to occasional supplemental water (Class II)
Foothill rainfall dependent (Class III)
Mountain rainfall dependent (Class III)
Uncultivable
Unsurveyed

Monte Albán

N

0   12
KILOMETERS

3.2 Monte Albán's estimated required agricultural catchment zone.

of several hundred square kilometers. In the next chapter, we look at this social catchment and its communities and discuss how they might have been incorporated into the Monte Albán system.

One might expect that a community would develop into an important center if it were located in a favorable environment that would attract immigrants and in which its population could produce a large surplus of food (see, e.g., Sanders and Nichols 1988). However, in the Valley of Oaxaca this is not what happened. No one lived at Monte Albán for more than 1,000 years of settled agricultural life, and it was hardly the best place for farming. Yet the abundance of Early I pottery tells us that Monte Albán was by far the largest site of that phase anywhere in the Valley of Oaxaca.

A rapidly growing population

Because this great Oaxacan city was continuously occupied for over a millennium, the remains of its earliest buildings, including those dating to Period I, have been either largely covered over with later construction or destroyed as older building materials were recycled. The imprint of this early period is not, however, entirely gone. Over time, numerous pottery fragments of the two Period I phases have been churned upward to the surface as a result of later construction and through natural processes such as animal burrowing and soil erosion. By studying the distributions of potsherds from various periods on the surface of the site, we are able to estimate where there was likely to have been human settlement during each ceramic phase.

Intensive survey of Monte Albán's surface remains has revealed three dense scatters of Early I sherds located near the top of the main north–south ridge, covering an area of 69 hectares. A less dense scatter of sherds was found over an additional 255 hectares, mostly in a zone extending north from the main ridge down to the base of the hill (fig. 3.3). From the area of distribution of Early I sherds (and estimating a population of about 25–50 persons per hectare, less for the area of more scattered pottery), we estimate a population for Early I of 3,500–7,000 (Blanton 1978:33–35) and take the middle value of about 5,000 as the best estimate of population for the period. Population growth continued into Late I, eventually reaching an estimated 17,000 (Blanton 1978:44)(fig. 3.4).

The Period I expansion of the city's population represents an estimated growth rate of 6 percent per year, a rate much higher than that of any of today's developing nations (Blanton, Kowalewski, Feinman, and Appel 1982:41). Although physical anthropological data pertaining to mortality (average age of death) and morbidity (health status) of past populations in the Valley of Oaxaca are scattered and incomplete, they suggest little in the way of a significant decrease in mortality or a change in health in the post-500 B.C. period (Hodges 1989). With mortality and health largely unchanged, population growth must have resulted from some combination of increased fertility and immigration. However, the growth rate of the city's population was too rapid to be accounted for solely by increased fertility (although high fertility may well have been a contributing factor). People must have migrated into the city in large numbers (Blanton, Finsten, Kowalewski, and Feinman 1996).

Some households probably moved to Monte Albán from San José Mogote, but that community's Rosario-phase population was only a little over 1,000, not enough to account for Monte Albán's total, and not every-

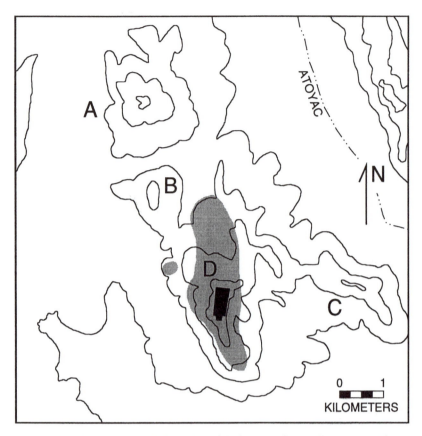

3.3 Distribution of Early I sherds from surface collections at Monte Albán.

one left there after the Rosario phase. In many other parts of the Valley of Oaxaca, Period I was a substantial growth phase; the number of sites increased from 72 for the Rosario phase to 259 for Early I and 643 for Late I (Kowalewski et al. 1989:ch. 4–6). Monte Albán's increase in population, then, was not generally at the expense of smaller communities. We conclude that Period I was a period of overall regional growth coupled with rural–urban migration. Some migrants to the city and the region may have come from outside the valley. However, if migrants with diverse cultural backgrounds came into the valley during Period I, their ethnic identities are not obvious to us in terms of either material culture or recognizable physical anthropological traits. Clearly, if there were migrants from more distant regions, they must have rapidly become acculturated into the valley's material-cultural system.

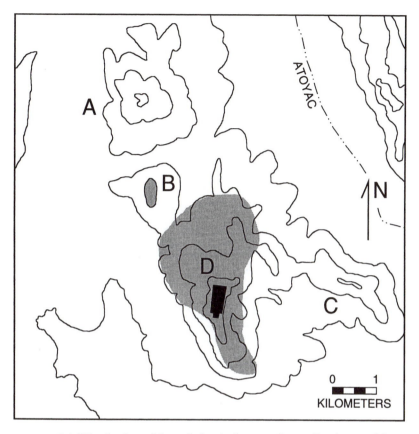

3.4 Distribution of Late I sherds from surface collections at Monte Albán.

The development of a new capital was one of several key demographic changes that occurred in the Valley of Oaxaca during this transition. Monte Albán eclipsed San José Mogote as the region's largest community. Many households increased in family size, and higher fertility, perhaps lower age at marriage, and migration all contributed to a more rapid rate of household formation, which significantly increased the production and consumption of economic goods.

Overall, Period I was a dynamic, rapid-growth demographic regime that contrasted markedly with the nearly stationary population that had characterized the area throughout the Early and Middle Formative. No Mesoamerican community of this or prior times is known to have grown so quickly, and no known Mesoamerican community of that time had reached this population size. It is therefore reasonable to propose that

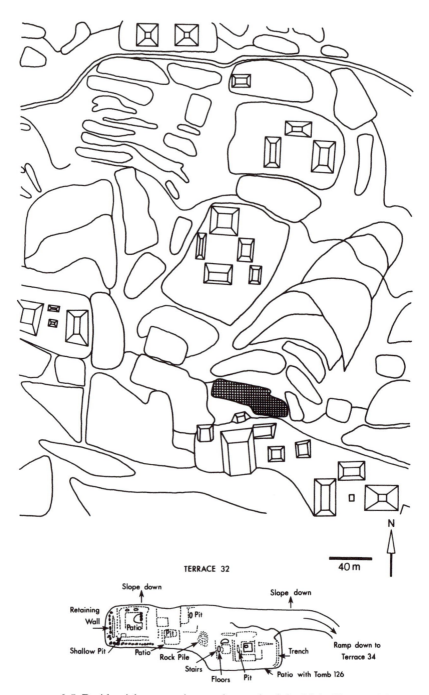

TERRACE 32

40 m

N

Slope down

Slope down

Retaining
Wall

Patio

Pit

Pit

Shallow Pit

Patio

Rock Pile

Stairs

Floors

Pit

Ramp down to
Terrace 34

Trench

Patio with Tomb 126

3.5 Residential terraces just to the north of the Main Plaza, at Monte
Albán, some of them containing mounded buildings arranged around
plazas. An ancient road is visible near the top of the figure, passing by a

Monte Albán's growth reflects Mesoamerica's first instance of an "urban revolution." It was, admittedly, a small-scale one. The populations we estimate for the new center, 5,000 inhabitants in Early I and 17,000 in Late I, are considerably smaller than those of later major cities such as Teotihuacan, around 200,000 persons during the Classic (Millon 1973), and Tenochtitlan, which also had 200,000 inhabitants. Monte Albán's population growth may seem almost insignificant to us now, accustomed as we are to cities of as many as 20 million, but the ancient world's cities were much smaller than today's. For example, in 1749, New York City, one of the largest settlements in North America north of Mexico, had a population of just over 13,000 (Chandler and Fox 1974:178). No world city exceeded 1 million persons until Beijing did so about A.D. 1800 (Chandler and Fox 1974:323).

In spite of the comparatively small numbers of people involved, it is important to recognize Period I as an instance of urban revolution. Prior to Monte Albán, San José Mogote was the largest community in the Valley of Oaxaca and the entire southern highlands with a total population estimated at roughly 1,000 persons. Monte Albán's rapid growth to five times that number must have been a striking departure from past experience. This growth would have created new problems that required the creative social and technological solutions we associate with the growth of urban settlements elsewhere. How was society going to provision not 1,000 people living on good land but 5,000 people perched on a high hill in a less-than-auspicious situation for farming? What about the inevitable disputes arising from crowding, limited access to land, public health problems, fresh water, and the removal of waste? Monte Albán's growth presented new kinds of challenges that would call for additional societal changes.

The nature of the early center and its functions

Most people at Monte Albán lived in houses similar to rural houses of the time (Winter 1974)(fig. 3.5). They were freestanding rectangular structures with one or more rooms, each room ranging in size between about 3 by 5 meters to about 4 by 6 meters. These are small dwellings likely to have housed nuclear families. Outside the house was an open area averaging about 300 square meters (or 10 meters in radius) in which

Caption for fig. 3.5 (*cont*)
terrace with two mounded buildings. The stippled terrace (Terrace 32) at the bottom is shown enlarged below, with details of partially excavated house remains visible on the surface. Based on Blanton (1978:fig.A.X-14) and Blanton, Kowalewski, Feinman, and Finsten (1993:fig.3.18).

3.6 Aztec house, showing a wedding ceremony (the couple is shown "tying the knot"). Adapted from Berdan and Anawalt (1997: folio 61r).

archaeologists encounter features including storage pits, burials, and ovens (Winter 1974). Domestic artifacts include grinding stones (metates) and their hand stones (manos), chipped stone tools, shell ornaments, and ceramic figurines and vessels (Winter 1974). Such assemblages indicate a normal range of household functions as we know these from rural sites of this and earlier periods.

Minor changes did occur in the Period I transformation that are evident in the Monte Albán houses. One was a switch from wattle-and-daub construction to more substantial construction using stone foundations and mud-brick walls (see fig. 3.7 and box 7). Similar houses were being constructed in other communities during Period I (Whalen

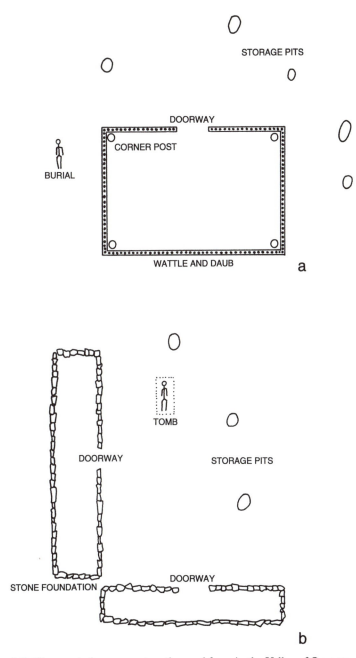

3.7 Changes in house construction and form in the Valley of Oaxaca: *a*. Early Formative house; *b*. Late I house with tomb.

Box 7   *The evolution of houses in the Valley of Oaxaca's Formative period*

Mesoamerican houses display certain consistent patterns while varying to some degree in size, number of rooms, building materials, and decorative elaboration from region to region and over time. Square or rectangular form was common, as were one-room houses (e.g., fig. 3.6), although houses with multiple rooms were sometimes built (e.g., Smith 1996a:fig. 6.8). This basic floor plan was already present in the Valley of Oaxaca by the Early Formative. During the San José phase, houses were built of wattle and daub, usually consisted of one room (sometimes with an outbuilding), and were free-standing structures located in the middle of open yards containing pit features for storage, burial, and cooking (e.g., Winter 1976)(fig. 3.7a). By Late I houses were frequently of mud-brick construction, some with stone foundations; were more likely to consist of multiple rooms situated at right angles to one another; partially enclosing patios; were freestanding as before but with smaller yards; made less use of domestic pit storage; and were more likely to have stone-lined, multichambered tombs under the patio floor (Whalen 1988; Winter 1974) (fig. 3.7b).

Drawing on this information on change in houses in the Valley of Oaxaca as well as Blanton's (1994) cross-cultural comparative study of houses and households, we reach several provisional conclusions regarding the significance of changing house form. (1) The decline in household storage indicates an increased dependence on markets or other social mechanisms for daily grain and other food supplies. (2) The transition from an open exterior yard to a partially enclosed interior patio may reflect an increasing interest in creating private domestic space within the partially enclosed patio spaces; in later periods, patios were even more completely enclosed (Winter 1974). This may indicate that households were more tightly integrated, discrete, and independent social units in Late I than they had been previously (Whalen 1988:267; cf. Drennan and Flannery 1983:70, who note an increase in "husband and wife" burials after the San José phase). (3) Although the replacement of single-room with multiroom houses may indicate the growth of larger, more complex extended households (Whalen 1988:268–69), it also may be a strategy for the communication of social status. Household status may be reflected not only in the number of rooms in a house and the quality of building materials but also in the degree of separation of living and entertaining areas from storage, food preparation, and other room functions (Blanton 1994:table 3–3). The separation of room functions, therefore, may have been one strategy for the communication of social standing during Late I. Whatever its function in society, change in house form is one more indicator of increasing complexity in Period I.

1981:88–105), yet Monte Albán houses were somewhat more densely packed than those in other communities of the period. Judging from the smaller sizes of storage pits on average for Early I than for earlier phases (Winter 1974:982), perhaps Monte Albán's residents stored somewhat less food. In later periods, storage pits are not found (Winter 1974:983), probably indicating that households obtained their daily food supply from markets or through governmental institutions. Generally, however, for Period I most migrants to the new city apparently carried with them their basic domestic institutions and functions, including their preference for freestanding nuclear-family dwellings surrounded by open yards.

Although the data are limited, the center was not populated predominantly by households of either extremely low or high socioeconomic status. Moving to the city did not entail a radical change in either domestic structure or function.

The pattern of community partition (barrios) identified at San José Mogote is apparent at Monte Albán from the beginning; houses continued to be clustered in barrio divisions throughout the city's long history (Blanton 1978:44–46). However, the dual division of San José Mogote was never replicated at Monte Albán. Instead the city always had more than two subdivisions, and in later periods it had as many as fifteen. In Early I, the surface distribution of sherds suggests three main clusters of houses near the top of the main hill, surrounding a large, relatively open flat space that was a civic-ceremonial area. Because the new Monte Albán system had integrated what had been three distinct valley polities, it is intriguing to consider the possibility that the three barrios represented households that had migrated to the new capital from the outlying polities. In later periods Monte Albán's barrios sometimes had distinctive ceramic assemblages that can be linked to separate subregions of the valley (see, e.g., Kowalewski et al. 1989:ch. 7). Although the design motifs on the Early I pottery vary stylistically between the three barrios (Blanton 1978:37–39), we have not yet been able to link these variations to discrete areas of the valley.

Apart from the excavation of a few houses, we know little about the city's people and their activities. We think that elite families lived at Monte Albán in houses elevated on stone and mud-brick platforms; such structures pertaining to this and earlier periods have been excavated elsewhere in the valley. The civic-ceremonial area in the midst of the three main concentrations of Early I sherds provides a critical perspective on Monte Albán's urban functions. Over the course of the city's occupation, this area, called the Main Plaza, was substantially flattened and architecturally modified into a vast civic-ceremonial concourse measuring approximately 250 meters by 100 meters, surrounded by massive pyramid platforms. As early as Period I, the area already served a civic-ceremonial role, as it was only here, so far as we can tell, that there were large structures that apparently had nonresidential functions. Deep inside a major, later platform on the north edge of the Main Plaza (the North Platform) was a partial structure dating to Early I with serpent motifs formed in stucco (Acosta 1965:816). By Late I, a large platform 2 meters high was taking shape over it. Because of the tremendous amount of later construction, the function of neither building can be determined (by the end of the construction sequence, in Period IIIB, 9 meters of fill had been added over the Early I structure). Another Period I structure that was partially exposed along the west edge of the plaza features a 6-meter-high wall constructed of large stones and rubble masonry columns.

Some 150 meters south of this wall is one of the Main Plaza's most important and revealing structures. This is the so-called Danzantes Gallery, a platform whose plaza-facing walls consisted of rows of carved stone slabs (Acosta 1965:814–16; Marcus 1976; Scott 1978). These carved monuments depict individuals in odd, dancelike poses, hence the orginal name for the building. But the building's purpose was not to display dancing figures; Michael Coe (1977:81) points to the gallery's purpose when he says that the "distorted pose of the limbs, the open mouth and closed eyes indicate that these are corpses... In many individuals, the genitals are clearly delineated, usually the stigma laid on captives in Mesoamerica, where nudity was considered scandalous. Furthermore, there are cases of sexual mutilation depicted on some *Danzantes*, blood streaming in flowery patterns from the severed part." This was a massive public display of what are likely to have been war captives. The builders of Monte Albán brought with them to their new location a kind of militaristic communicative medium in carved stone first developed during the Rosario phase at San José Mogote, where the earliest such figure was erected, also in a very public place. But in Period I Monte Albán this theme was greatly elaborated, necessitating the construction of a special building that could hold numerous figures (over 300 *danzantes* are known).

Monte Albán as a disembedded capital

Considering location, size, and functions, we regard Period I Monte Albán as the capital of the Valley of Oaxaca region. To this point we have discussed several lines of evidence that support this contention.

1. In relation to other communities in the Valley of Oaxaca, Monte Albán stands out for the rather sudden appearance of an unprecedented number of people in a setting that is unexpected for farmers. By contrast, during the long sequence of human habitation that preceded its founding, valley communities had tended to be located near high-quality deep soil and water sources that could be tapped for irrigation agriculture.

2. It was the only community in the region that could not have come close to producing its own food supply from its agricultural catchment. The city's founders likely did not expect a large proportion of the community's population to engage in farming, and they knew that they could depend on a supply of labor to carry water, food, and other materials to hilltop consumers.

3. The city grew faster and became more populous than any other

community of this or any earlier period. The next-largest communities in
Early I, either San José Mogote or Yegüih, had fewer than 1,000 persons,
while Monte Albán's population topped 5,000. The discrepancy between
the population of Monte Albán and the second-ranking centers was even
greater during Late I. Whereas the latter's population was over 17,000,
the next-largest places had only 1,400–1,900 inhabitants.

4. No other site in the valley had a ceremonial concourse and public
architecture as large as Monte Alban's, and only Monte Albán had a
Danzantes Gallery. We infer that it functioned as a regional center where
important ceremonial activities were carried out on a scale larger than at
any other site and where the military successes of a regional-scale polity
were publicly displayed.

Monte Albán's environmental, demographic, and functional unique-
ness supports the inference that it was established as the political capital
of the region at the beginning of Period I. What might have been the
reasons for this? Because there are no textual accounts (known written
texts are few and primarily indicate the names of deceased persons
depicted in the Danzantes Gallery), we must approach this question indi-
rectly. Fortunately, there are many possible analogs of Period I Monte
Albán in the literature on ancient and modern cities.

The best-known region in which early city formation is elucidated by
textual sources is ancient Greece, where political change was often
reflected by changes in settlement patterns. The process of political
consolidation generally referred to as synoecism could involve the
foundation, movement, or expansion of political capitals (Demand 1990;
cf. Marcus and Flannery 1996:ch. 11). In political synoecism, previously
autonomous villages or even whole ethnic groups accepted the dominance of a single political center without relocating to that center. One
example occurred in the eighth century B.C. in Attica when a capital for
the region was established at Athens (Snodgrass 1980:34). In physical
synoecism, the populations involved in the consolidation move to a new
political center, either by choice or by force (Demand 1990). The political center in question could be an existing center or a new one built
specifically to symbolize the new political order. It might be built at some
distance, as in the case of a colony, or relocated within the traditional
domain in a place better suited to its political purpose. It is of interest that
even in the case of Athens, population was eventually concentrated in the
city, so that political synoecism led eventually to physical synoecism
(Snodgrass 1980:34).

In some cases, the reasons for synoecism are not entirely clear. The
foundation of Athens occurred prior to historical writing and is therefore
not well described. Later writers refer to it as a political coming together,

or federation, of previously autonomous groups (Hignett 1958:34). Among the many examples that occurred later than that of Athens, however, the major reason appears to have been a strategy of political reorganization for military defense (Demand 1990). In these examples, urban relocation as military synoecism was carried out to organize a polity for defense against a major invader – Athens, the Persians, Sparta, or another major power. In one example, "the Deinomenid tyrants of Sicily used [physical synoecism] to create formidable instruments of power that enabled them to defeat the Carthaginian threat while creating a power base for their own rule" (Demand 1990:45).

Did a process analogous to synoecism occur in Period I in the Valley of Oaxaca? Judging from the *danzantes*, early Monte Albán had an interest in military affairs, but the type of synoecism described for Greece probably was not entirely responsible for the new Period I capital. No known group inside or outside the Valley of Oaxaca would have posed a military threat on the scale of the Persians, the Athenians, or the Carthaginians. Period I Monte Albán was the only large-scale polity in the southern highlands. Even beyond that area, no known polity was large enough to represent such a threat. Monte Albán would in fact have been a major military power vis-à-vis smaller polities in the southern highlands, and researchers are now identifying their synoecisms in response to it.

Yet certain aspects of the synoecism model seem applicable. Monte Albán's growth can be understood by reference to military problems that may have faced the residents of the Valley of Oaxaca. Mountain dwellers coming down to raid villages in the agricultually superior valley might have been a persistent problem that could have been more effectively dealt with through a unified political structure. Even small-scale social formations can at times present a formidable problem if they temporarily organize for a military campaign. In 1580, for example, the Western Mixe organized for long enough to mount an attack on the mountain Zapotec of the Cajones Valley that required colonial authorities to send in a force aided by 2,000 Mixtec auxiliaries. However, we have not yet found evidence of enough people in the mountains around the valley who even collectively would have posed such a threat in the Rosario phase or Early I (Finsten 1996). A better but still speculative possibility of a significant external threat is raiding campaigns launched from other chiefdoms in Puebla, Morelos, Veracruz, the Mixteca Alta, or the Isthmus of Tehuantepec. A unified polity at Monte Albán would have been able to respond to external threats of these kinds while at the same time reducing the amount of intramural warfare between the valley's communities and increasing the potential for interaction among them. As we describe later in chapter 5, Mesoamerica around 500 B.C. must have been a politically

unpredictable place. Every regional society was undergoing reorganization, if not upheaval. A centralized or confederated regional government
would have had advantages of scale beyond the purely military in diplomacy, power, prestige, and intelligence gathering. Thus, the foundation of
Monte Albán is probably understandable in relation to a situation more
complex than just one major external enemy.

Although the dominant process involved in Greek synoecism, military
defense from a major enemy, probably is not a fully satisfactory analogy,
we are still intrigued by the Athenian case, which was a federation of polities rather than a purely defensive strategy. Again, we do not know the
specifics of why a federation was developed in Athenian politics, but we
think that a federation or coalition may have played a role in the Valley of
Oaxaca. We suggest that the best model might be a particular category of
federation in which regional-scale social unity is based on what is called a
"disembedded capital." This odd phrase refers to a situation where a
decision is made to strengthen linkages between autonomous or partially
autonomous local polities through the creation or elaboration of a multi-
centered regional-scale polity. One strategy is to build a new capital in a
neutral location apart from the participating centers and their local
domains (i.e., disembedded from the existing settlement pattern).
Neutrality is a key feature of this strategy. Because the aim is to develop a
regional rather than a local political system, the region's capital cannot be
thought of as representing in its entirety the culture, polity, or economy of
any one of the constituent parts. Instead, it must be able to transcend
local differences in the construction of a broader, more inclusive, larger-
scale social system.

Many examples of the disembedded-capital strategy are known from
both ancient and more recent times. We need not go any farther than
Washington, D.C., to find a well-described example (e.g., Bowling 1991;
Walton 1966). Charged with founding a new national capital for the
federation of the United States of America, George Washington chose a
site on the Potomac River. The Potomac, Washington reasoned, was a
"conjunction of all things" for the new polity, a neutral location exactly at
the midpoint geographically between the northern and southern states
(Walton 1966:7–8). By balancing the agricultural slave economy of the
south with the business economy of the north, the new capital would
serve to unite a country. Similarly, in Canada, Ottawa was chosen as the
neutral site of federal government that could help to unite a country torn
by the dualism of French and English provinces (Knight 1977a, b).
Canberra was selected as a site for the capital of an Australian federation
that could resolve the conflict between the provincial capitals of Sydney
and Melbourne; New Delhi's location, near the Hindu/Muslim border,

"removed politics from the dominating port capitals, Bombay and Calcutta" (Fischer 1984:9). The Hague seated government away from the rival Amsterdam and Rotterdam (Fischer 1984:9). Brasília, similarly, integrated a Brazil that contained the competing centers of Rio de Janeiro and São Paulo (Epstein 1973:28–30). Even ancient Jerusalem illustrates the importance of regional disembeddedness; as related by Guthe (1959:132), with "the capture of the Jebusite fortress Jerusalem fell into David's hands. . . he was thus placed in contact with the northern tribes . . . [this] stronghold became the capital of his kingdom, a place belonging neither to Judah nor to the northern tribes, and therefore neutral."

Monte Albán, located centrally with respect to the Valley of Oaxaca, seems to illustrate the principle of the disembedded capital. It was founded in a location not obviously controlled by any prior polity and therefore would have been politically neutral. Its environmentally marginal location would not have threatened any existing claims to valuable agricultural land or other economic resources, and since a regional capital is supported by tribute it need not support itself agriculturally. In this kind of situation, environmental marginality might even be an advantage for a new capital. Brasília, built in the middle of a tropical forest, was placed similarly without regard to any local resource base.

In all the cases of disembedded capitals mentioned above, where conflicting local interests and traditions threatened the vitality of a regional polity or even its continued existence, a decision was made to intensify regional integration. Although the Valley of Oaxaca did become more fragmented regionally during the Rosario phase, we cannot be sure just what were viewed as the major advantages of intensified regional integration. We suggest, however, that a reduction of intraregional conflict coupled with an increased potential for intraregional interaction would have been among the major payoffs of a more inclusive system.

Monte Albán in the Mesoamerican world

Understanding Monte Albán's founding will require that we look beyond the local situation to take into consideration the important long-distance interactions laid out earlier. Viewed from the scale of the southern highlands and beyond, an integrated regional society in the Valley of Oaxaca would have had the advantage of being able to improve its military and diplomatic potential for external warfare, not so much to defend against any particular major enemy as to respond more effectively to threats posed by an increasingly chaotic, militaristic world. Data from several other Mesoamerican localities point strongly in the direction of a restructuring taking place on a scale beyond that of the Valley of Oaxaca during

Period I. These changes include an apparent increase in the intensity of warfare. An additional factor is that a consolidated regional government with its military command at Monte Albán would have been in a more favorable position to regularize the flows of goods exchanged over long distances. As the Valley of Oaxaca increasingly assumed the status of core zone in an emerging core-periphery system, it would have seen an increase in the importation of goods from outside (for example, obsidian), and perhaps increasing competition from other aspiring core-zone actors for these same goods. We have evidence from our archaeological surveys of a change in the nature of regional boundaries at the fringes of the Valley of Oaxaca at this time, including the establishment of a new kind of site that appears to have played a role in regional boundary maintenance. The establishment of these boundary sites at the same time that the region was achieving a new level of regional social and economic integration suggests a likely causal relationship between social change at the level of inter-regional interactions and local political evolution.

4   The great transformation

Now that we have looked in some detail at Monte Albán, we can investigate the broader consequences of its founding for people throughout the Valley of Oaxaca. The decision to establish a new capital seems to have set in motion a series of profound social changes in the region that probably were not entirely anticipated by those who had worked in favor of change or those who had followed or been forced to accept it. In the most general terms, the social system of the valley during Period I increased in scale, integration, complexity, and boundedness (Blanton et al. 1993:13–18). Scale refers to size, including more people and more human settlements. Integration indicates the number and kinds of social interactions and interdependencies between persons and groups. The evolution of the Monte Albán state, which fostered the dissolution of the old polity boundaries of the Rosario phase, resulted in an increased amount of social interaction over the entire region. Complexity refers to the number of unlike parts in a social formation or system and includes such features as specialized production and hierarchical differences between social segments (for example, status and power differences between individuals, groups, and communities). Boundedness refers to flows of materials, information, and people in and out of the region; boundedness increases with greater regulation and control of cross-boundary flows. Changes in scale, integration, complexity, and boundedness in the Valley of Oaxaca add up to a significant episode of sociocultural evolution. In this chapter, we look at what this sociocultural evolution meant in terms of changes in specific sites, social groups, types of specializations, technology, and other transitions. We start with one aspect of social complexity, the growth of hierarchy, because it is one of the most conspicuous variables in this great transformation.

The evolution of hierarchy

Hierarchy refers to a system of levels ranked one above the other, and rule or control in which higher levels dominate lower ones. Between 600 B.C.

and 100 B.C., the society of the Valley of Oaxaca increased in size – meaning numbers of people and numbers of inhabited places. At the same time, its human hierarchy expanded in number of levels, the differences between them, and even the diversity of people at the same level.

In complex societies, all sorts of activities are hierarchically organized. Restaurants have dishwashers, maître d's, head chefs, owners; major-league baseball teams not only have distinctions among levels on the field – batboys, players, coaches, managers, and owners – but also stadium and marketing operations that have their own hierarchies. Not all social activities are hierarchically organized in such formal or permanent ways. Nomadic hunter-gatherers such as the San, the Inuit, and presumably the people of Mesoamerica before 2000 B.C. had more flexible and shifting ways of getting things done in which leadership roles were neither so much attached to a person nor so easily distinguished from those of followers. Sometimes small groups in complex societies can be resolutely democratic and nonhierarchical too.

Location in space and the physical settings of hierarchical positions matter a great deal. Places are important or central if the people who occupy them can collect things or information easily (compare the maître d' with the dishwasher, for example). Bosses symbolize their style of rule by their location in space. For example, some major league baseball owners may be found regularly in the bleachers in center field, in the field-level box next to the dugout, or in the sky box; others are never at the stadium at all. In societies that stress more egalitarian principles, leaders submerge their personae in the common life and are distinguished neither by the trappings of office nor by special location.

As archaeologists we looked for and found an abundance of material evidence for hierarchy in the Valley of Oaxaca. Here we consider three specific domains of hierarchy (see Kowalewski et al. 1989): settlement, civic-ceremonial, and status and wealth. The settlement hierarchy is the set of all the cities, towns, villages, hamlets, and isolated residences in a region. This hierarchy orders a range of different activities (including government, marketing, and temple activities) and organizes them on the landscape. The more functions or activities that take place in a settlement, the larger its population will be; in other words, a settlement's population size reflects its functional size. The civic-ceremonial hierarchy reflects levels of political control. We may not be able to separate "religion" from "government" in Oaxaca (perhaps because rulers performed both functions), but we can identify a hierarchy of very specific places in which political control was exercised. Change in the civic-ceremonial hierarchy is central to our concern with the rise of the state in Oaxaca.

Finally, the hierarchy of status and wealth is known from excavations of houses, tombs, and other burials.

Settlement hierarchy

To reconstruct the hierarchy of inhabited places in the Valley of Oaxaca and how it changed over time required several kinds of information.

1. We needed units that could be ranked; these are the remains of past settlements – spatially bounded, inhabited places that we discovered and mapped during the course of our archaeological surveys. We refer to them as archaeological sites. We had to find and locate all of the region's sites so that we could feel confident that we had discovered all the settlements in the ranks above the smallest inhabited places. Missing just a few of the higher-ranked places could have severely distorted the picture.

2. We had to be sure that the study area included every settlement that was part of the past system of places. It would not do to simply select a study area arbitrarily, potentially excluding places that also were part of the regional society. If we were constructing a settlement hierarchy for the United States, for example, we would do well to include California and, since national boundaries may be irrelevant for many activities, perhaps Toronto, Vancouver, and the border cities of northern Mexico. In our case, we can show that the Valley of Oaxaca was a highly self-contained region in terms of day-to-day dependence and interaction; any valley center was only half a day's walk at most from each of its nearest neighbors, while the closest settlements outside the valley were a day's walk or more away across the rugged terrain of the mountains that border the valley.

3. We needed a single criterion for comparing the places so that they could be ranked in a consistent manner. We chose population size, because cross-culturally this variable is a good measure of the overall importance of a place (see, e.g., Haggett 1966:114–18). To estimate the past population sizes of the archaeological sites, we used a method that has been applied in several regions of highland Mesoamerica (see box 8).

4. We had to know the boundaries of the settlements and their estimated populations for each archaeological time period. Survey crews used the different pottery forms and styles to trace the limits of inhabited areas for each time phase separately; we then measured each site and made population estimates for each phase.

5. We had to identify hierarchical levels. We therefore displayed the populations of the settlements for each period in a histogram in which the horizontal axis gives the population sizes of the settlements (smallest to the left and largest to the right) and the vertical axis shows how many settlements there were at each population-size interval. In hierarchical

---

Box 8 *Estimating past population size*

Systematic archaeological settlement pattern survey is a means of estimating human population growth over broad geographic regions. Survey-based population estimates, while not as precise as modern census data, are clearly the best method that archaeologists have for tracing the population history of periods for which census information is unavailable.

The most detailed, large-scale archaeological research on past population trends has been carried out in Mesoamerica, especially the Basin of Mexico (Sanders, Parsons, and Santley 1979) and the Valley of Oaxaca (Feinman et al. 1985; Kowalewski et al. 1989). Regional archaeological surveys in highland Mexico (including the surveys we conducted in Oaxaca) use two standard ways of estimating past population. At sites where we can still see house foundations or house lots on the surface, we estimate or count the number of houses and multiply by the average number of persons per house. Since we do not know how large pre-Hispanic households were, we substitute a figure from historical and recent times in Mesoamerica, five to ten persons per house (e.g., Blanton 1978:29–30). Generally, however, individual houses are no longer visible on the surface, especially in areas now under cultivation. We can, however, measure the size of ancient settlements in land area on the basis of the surface distribution of pottery sherds and then multiply the measured area for each phase by estimated ranges of the density of persons per hectare derived from the settlement density of highland Mesoamerican communities of historical and recent times (Parsons 1971:23; Sanders 1965:50). Surveyors typically employ an estimate of ten to twenty-five persons per hectare for most settlements (Blanton, Kowalewski, Feinman, and Appel 1982:10–12). For a few communities where surface artifacts are extremely dense, an estimate of up to one hundred persons per hectare has been used.

Regional population estimates based on archaeological surveys cannot be considered completely accurate. For example, site boundaries for some periods may be difficult to establish with certainty, especially for multiperiod sites in which several phases share certain long-surviving pottery types. Also, our archaeological periods in most cases lasted more than a hundred years; not all sites dating to a particular period were necessarily occupied contemporaneously. Although the population numbers must be considered estimates, archaeological survey data certainly do provide a relative index of temporal trends and spatial distributions of past populations.

---

systems, ranked units never have a normal, bell-shaped statistical distribution, since there are always many more small units or communities than large ones. Because of this pattern, there are no handy statistical formulas for automatically determining how many levels there were and where to draw the upper and lower limits of each level. To do so requires making assumptions about the form of the hierarchy, which is what we are trying to learn about in the first place. Therefore the process of identifying hierarchical levels is somewhat subjective and involves looking for natural breaks in the histogram. Although archaeologists might argue over the details of how to interpret these histograms, the main patterns of the time span in question are clear (figs. 4.1–4.3).

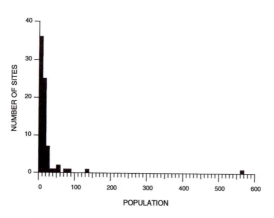

4.1 Rosario-phase site-size histogram for the Oaxaca and Ejutla Valleys.

The Rosario-phase histogram for the Oaxaca and Ejutla Valleys (fig. 4.1) reveals one large settlement, San José Mogote. The next-largest site (Yegüih), with a population estimate of 132, was much smaller and can probably be grouped with several settlements of slightly smaller population (81, 70, 54, 53, 48, etc.). Below this middle range there are a large number of small hamlets and isolated residences. Because the Rosario-phase sites were typically occupied intensively in later times, our site size and population estimates are quite crude, but it seems clear that there were at least two distinct hierarchical levels above the smallest inhabited places.

Figure 4.4 shows the distribution of settlements of the top two levels in the Rosario phase. The northern, Etla arm of the valley was dominated by San José Mogote. The eastern and southern arms each had at least two sites of the second rank. There were apparently no Rosario-phase sites in the center of the valley and certainly no large sites of that time period. This uninhabited zone suggests relatively little contact and interdependence among people in the three valley arms.

The Early I settlement hierarchy (fig. 4.2) has three and perhaps four levels, not including the 258 places with populations of 90 or less. In Early I there were 21 places with populations greater than 100, while in the Rosario phase there were only 2. When plotted on the map (fig. 4.5), the top-level places of Early I form a hub-and-spoke pattern centered on the largest center, Monte Albán.

The histogram for Late I (fig. 4.3) suggests at least three and perhaps as many as five levels above the numerous smallest hamlets (five levels are represented in fig. 4.6). The central part of the valley has much more settlement in Late I than it did earlier, but other parts of the region also

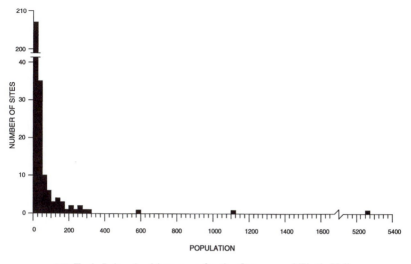

4.2 Early I site-size histogram for the Oaxaca and Ejutla Valleys.

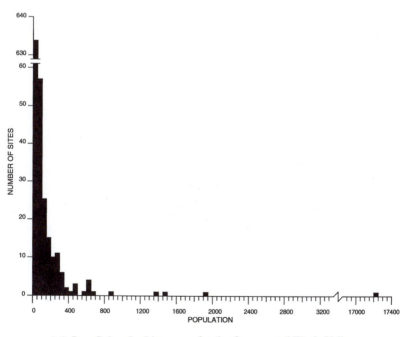

4.3 Late I site-size histogram for the Oaxaca and Ejutla Valleys.

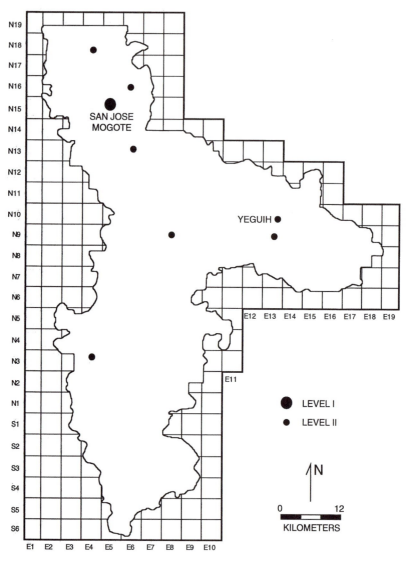

4.4 Rosario-phase settlements, showing the locations of sites in the top two levels of the population hierarchy.

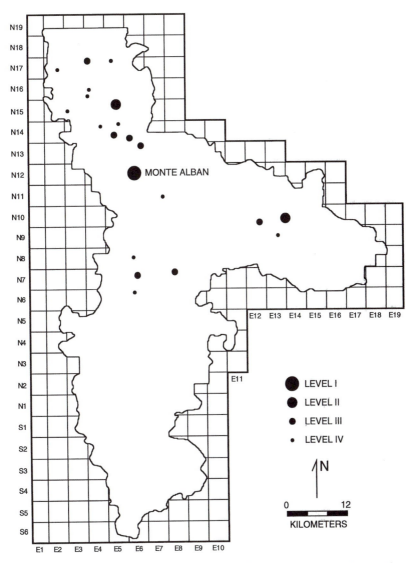

4.5 Early I settlements, showing the locations of sites in the top four levels of the population hierarchy.

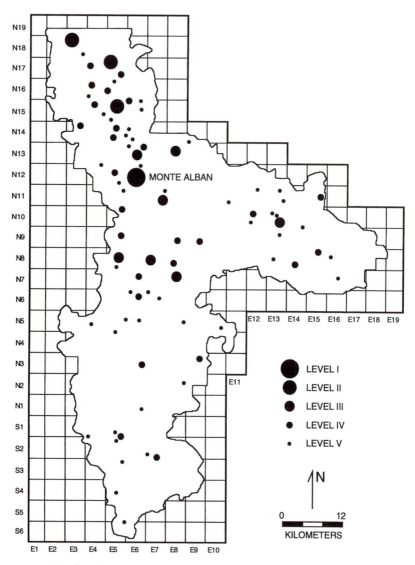

4.6 Late I settlements, showing the locations of sites in the top five levels of the population hierarchy.

increased in population density. Given the decline in average distance between the settlements of this growing system by comparison with earlier periods, the valley can be said to have been more integrated as a whole in Late I.

No matter how one counts the levels, the hierarchy clearly became deeper overtime; there were more levels in Late I than in the Rosario phase. There always was only one top-ranked place, but each successive phase added more sites to the middle levels of the hierarchy, and the range and midpoint of each level increased as well. For example, the midpoint for second-level places in the Rosario phase was 90. In Early I, a settlement had to have close to 600 people to be included in the second level; by Late I it had to have more than 1,300.

The top-level place increased in population almost tenfold from Rosario to Early I and then tripled again by the end of Late I. The middle ranks expanded as well. Places larger than small hamlets but not as large as the top center increased almost fourfold from Rosario to Early I and three and a half times again from Early I to Late I. The total population living in these middle-ranking centers increased over ten times from Rosario to Early I and another four and a half times from Early I to Late I. At no other time in its history has Oaxaca society undergone such a radical change in its settlement hierarchy.

The civic-ceremonial hierarchy

To analyze the civic-ceremonial hierarchy, we asked the same questions we did for the settlement hierarchy: what are the units to be ranked, how are they to be compared, how is the universe bounded in space, how is it bounded in time, and how do we determine hierarchical levels?

In Mesoamerica, public buildings were constructed on raised platforms (Marquina 1964) (fig. 4.7 and box 9). Elite residences, plazas, and carved stone monuments are also indicators of civic-ceremonial activities. Ideally we would have information on the ground plans, volumes, construction materials, and façades of public buildings, but these features of Rosario-phase and Period I constructions have long since been covered up or removed by later pre-Hispanic construction. The best we can do is to count the mounds and plazas and the carved stone monuments. The universe of public architecture relevant to this discussion is limited to the Oaxaca and Ejutla Valleys. Specifying the time of construction or use of monumental architecture is more difficult, since we are usually reduced to using potsherds found on the surface, and pre-Hispanic construction crews are known to have moved fill (containing sherds and other refuse) from one place to another. Dating Rosario-phase construction is the most

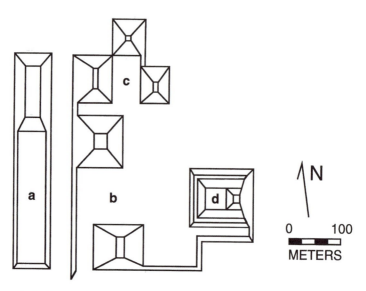

4.7 Public buildings at Roaló. Redrawn from Blanton, Kowalewski, Feinman, and Appel (1982: fig. A. XI-28).

difficult, because so many of the buildings were covered up or used later. Dating improves somewhat by Late I, because buildings from that era are more likely to be larger, nearer the surface, or the latest constructions to be built on a given site.

The best measures for studying and comparing the levels of the civic-ceremonial hierarchy are the numbers of mounds, the mound and plaza arrangements, and the presence of carved stone monuments. Twenty-four, or approximately one-third, of the Rosario-phase sites have mounds associated with Rosario pottery. San José Mogote has nine mounds, thirteen sites have two to eight mounds, and ten places have one mound each. At San José Mogote the most prominent buildings were rectangular, up to 28 meters on a side, elevated on platforms, and reached by broad stairways built of half-ton stone blocks (e.g., Marcus and Flannery 1996:126–31). Similar large blocks form stairways at Rosario-phase sites elsewhere in the valley. The surface survey and excavation evidence currently suggests a hierarchy of two or at most three levels above the places that had no apparent civic-ceremonial functions (fig. 4.8). San José Mogote was the leading place. About a dozen sites in the next level had multiple mounds. Each arm of the valley had at least two of the larger multiple-mound centers. Sites with single mounds are difficult to interpret in terms of the region's civic-ceremonial hierarchy. Throughout the Early and Middle Formative periods, a large proportion of sites had a

Box 9 *Public buildings in pre-Hispanic Oaxaca*

Public buildings and some elite houses in pre-Hispanic Mesoamerica typically were elevated on platforms (Marquina 1964). Their ruins are now mounds of earth and stone. We have mapped the surface remains of some 2,000 such mounded buildings in the Valley of Oaxaca, and other archaeologists have excavated a small sample of these buildings. Almost always, mounds fronted on, were arranged around, or were situated in plazas. Hence, the basic public architectural unit was an ordered space consisting of buildings built on mounds and a plaza (or plazas). Several typical mound/plaza arrangements are visible in the mound complex at the site of Roaló in the Valle Grande region (Blanton, Kowalewski, Feinman, and Appel 1982:appendix XI, p. 464). Here, a single mound fronts on an elongated plaza (a in fig. 4.7) open on three sides, while two mounds partially enclose a larger but also architecturally open plaza (b). By contrast, several mounds are arranged so as to nearly enclose and limit access to a smaller plaza (c). A plaza (d) with even more restricted access faces a small mound at the top of the larger structure and is reached only by two flights of stairs from plaza b.

Because so few of the valley's approximately 2,000 platform mounds have been excavated and fully published, we rarely know how a particular mound or mound complex was used, but the mound/plaza arrangements themselves can provide some glimpses into possible functions. Excavated elite houses (e.g., Bernal 1965:fig. 13; Caso, Bernal, and Acosta 1967:plan 10) consist of rooms on low platforms tightly enclosing a plaza space, allowing for restriction of traffic flow into domestic areas, similar to plaza c in Figure 4.7. We assume that more open mound/plaza arrangements, such as found with plazas a and b at Roaló (fig. 4.7), created open public spaces, possibly for ritual, or perhaps markets (Blanton 1989).

Mesoamerican platform mounds are not the Great Pyramids of Egypt – the work involved in their construction represented only a small fraction of total household labor available each year, and therefore mound building can hardly be considered as defining the nature of the Mesoamerican economy or society. But through comparisons of mound complexes in terms of their size and varied arrangements around plazas, public buildings can be a source for understanding the pre-Hispanic social systems of Oaxaca.

single mound and therefore we are not sure whether we should consider these to have been "centers."

What is not yet entirely clear is how integrated and complex this apparent hierarchy was. Was San José Mogote just like the other multiple-mound centers except larger, or did it have special functions? Given the presence of buffer zones between what appear to have been discrete polities, it is unlikely that San José Mogote was the valley's political capital during the Rosario phase. Instead, it is likely that each valley arm or subregion had at least one political center, each with subordinate centers that had their own civic-ceremonial architecture. San José Mogote was the political center for the Etla subregion, but it was larger and more important than the head towns in the other arms of the valley.

This civic-ceremonial hierarchy changed dramatically in Early I (fig. 4.9). More sites had the mounds indicative of public architecture, there

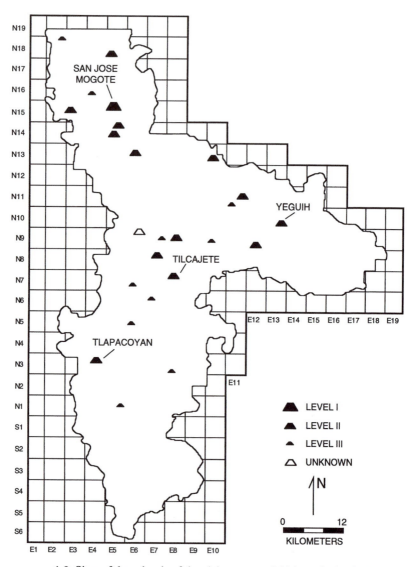

4.8 Sites of three levels of the civic-ceremonial hierarchy in the Rosario phase. Single-mound sites are shown as Level III.

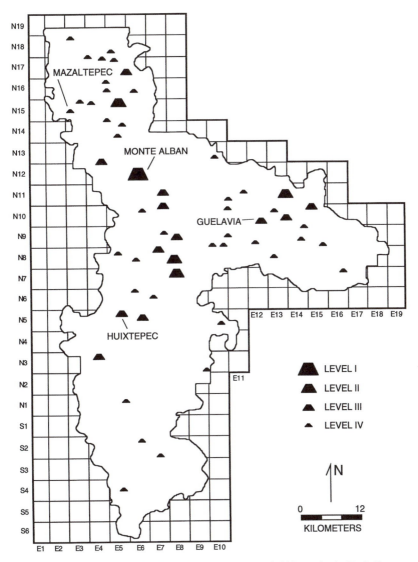

4.9 Sites of four levels of the civic-ceremonial hierarchy in Early I.

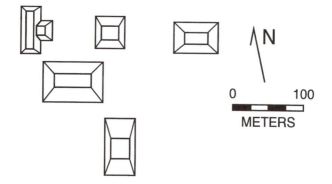

4.10 Public buildings at San Pablo Huixtepec. Redrawn from Blanton, Kowalewski, Feinman, and Appel (1982: fig. A.XI-46).

were more mounds, and mounds were often larger, all of which suggests that people were putting more effort into building and maintaining civic-ceremonial facilities. The proportions of sites that may have had mounds were similar for the Rosario phase and Early I, but Early I had three times the number of sites. Interestingly, virtually every local cluster of sites had some public architecture.

The civic-ceremonial hierarchy expanded in Early I. Not counting the sites without public architecture and sites with only one mound, we think that there was a four-level hierarchy. Monte Albán stood alone at the top, with its early structures under and near the North Platform, its huge Main Plaza, and its Danzantes Gallery. The second level had four places with ten to fourteen mounds (at least one site in each valley arm), the third level had twelve sites with five to seven mounds, and the fourth level had forty sites with two to four mounds. Because of later construction on top of these same buildings, our counts of the numbers of mounds should be treated as relative estimates. Only excavations can reveal the actual construction histories for each site. Yet Early I clearly had an expanded hierarchy of public building, with another level added in the middle and a more spectacular top tier.

This hierarchy did not just expand but became more complex. Obviously Monte Albán was different from the secondary centers; its civic-ceremonial buildings were not just local ones writ large. At the middle and lower levels of the hierarchy, too, there was variation in the forms and arrangements of buildings and plazas indicating differences in purpose. Of the five sites at which the Early I mounds could still be distinguished despite later building, two had only one mound each. Another, Santo Tomás Mazaltepec, situated at the western edge of the Etla arm of

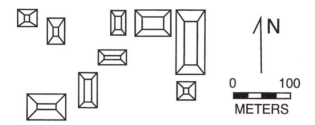

4.11 Public buildings at San Juan Guelavía. Redrawn from Kowalewski et al. (1989: fig. A.IX-45).

the valley, had a group of three mounds enclosing a large plaza measuring 49 by 35 meters. The plaza area was delimited by a wall. At San Pablo Huixtepec, near the southern edge of Early I settlement in the Valle Grande, there is another rectangular plaza, 50 meters on a side, loosely defined by three mounds (fig. 4.10). One further site that provides a relatively unobstructed view of Early I architecture is near San Juan Guelavía (fig. 4.11). This site has nine fairly scattered platforms, most of them quite large for the time. Six of the mounds seem to form a rectangular arrangement, open to the south, that would have made a very large, loosely defined plaza. Huixtepec and Guelavía appear to have planned layouts, and four of the five sites with fairly certain Early I architecture share the same orientation, 7–13° east of north. Most of the large population centers of Early I have mound arrangements that, prior to Late I or other later building activity, probably looked like those at Guelavía.

Public architecture and the civic-ceremonial hierarchy were further expanded and differentiated in Late I (fig. 4.12). That the hierarchy continued to grow in size and complexity during Period I is important to note, because later periods saw much reorganization but not nearly the same rate of expansion and differentiation. Whereas in the Rosario phase there were about fourteen sites with two or more platform mounds, Early I had fifty-seven and Late I had ninety-four. Late I had more distinguishable levels in the number-of-mounds-per-site histogram, with five as opposed to four in Early I (see box 10). The sites with the best-dated Late I architecture support this five-level hierarchy interpretation. This sample of sites illustrates that the total volume of construction and the sizes of plazas increase regularly with the position of these settlements in the civic-ceremonial hierarchy (Kowalewski et al. 1989: ch. 6). Top-level sites had larger volumes of platform-mound construction and larger plazas; centers with fewer mounds had smaller volumes of construction and smaller plazas.

In addition to increases in public architectural construction and the

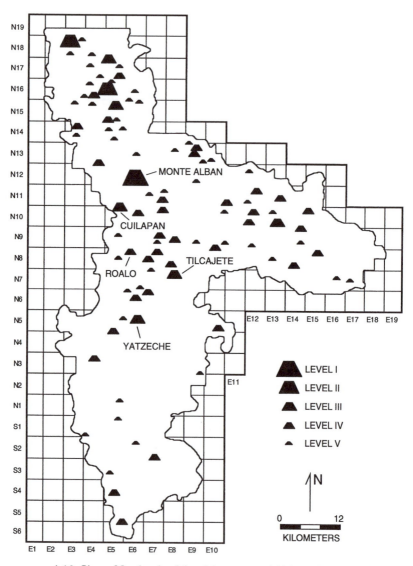

4.12 Sites of five levels of the civic-ceremonial hierarchy in Late I.

Box 10 *Civic-ceremonial hierarchy and state formation*

The changing hierarchy of population and civic-ceremonial centers not only reveals the growing complexity of the regional system during Period I but also may help us pinpoint the beginnings of the state. Information on the regional hierarchy of governing centers is crucial for the archaeological identification of states. Our data point to the two-level hierarchical structure of a chiefdom during the Rosario phase in the Valley of Oaxaca. By Late I, the civic-ceremonial hierarchy indicates the likelihood of as many as five hierarchical levels in governing centers, including a regional capital and a well-developed system of secondary centers governing districts within the valley arms. These data suggest there was a state form of governance in the valley by Late I. We suggest that the critical transition to a state form of governance occurred during Early I, when the establishment of a new capital at Monte Albán added a new top tier to the regional civic-ceremonial hierarchy.

---

evidence for more depth or vertical complexity in the civic-ceremonial hierarchy, two trends having to do with the complexity of the hierarchy become clear by Late I. Civic-ceremonial centers were more differentiated, with special types of architecture depending on what different roles a center played in the regional system. There also is clearer evidence for spatial or territorial administrative units; each valley arm was apparently divided into several component districts, each headed by a secondary center under the oversight of Monte Albán (fig. 4.13).

Because so few public buildings of Period I have been excavated, we know very little about how they were used. Some probably housed elite families (see, e.g., Whalen 1981:89–95), while others probably were temples or housed other kinds of official or ceremonial activities. Plazas were probably sites of ritual and perhaps commerce. A large, rectangular building, nearly square or with a width half its length, is one structure type, already present in the Rosario phase. Small rectangular buildings also are found. Yet another type of structure, amounting to 10 percent of all the measurable buildings at three sites in our sample of best-dated Late I sites, was longer and narrower than either of these and may have been a hall, perhaps reached by a broad stairway.

Distinct arrangements of mounds are found at sites at different levels of the civic-ceremonial hierarchy. Lower-level sites in this hierarchy have single, smaller plazas and simple clusters of mounds. Higher-level centers have larger plazas and complex arrangements of multiple clusters of mounds. The second through the fifth levels of the hierarchy also have an interesting spatial pattern. Sites located on the edge of the region or on boundaries between districts within the valley usually have tight, formal arrangements of mounds, such as the closed four-mound group. In contrast, sites in the interior of the valley have open, less formal arrangements

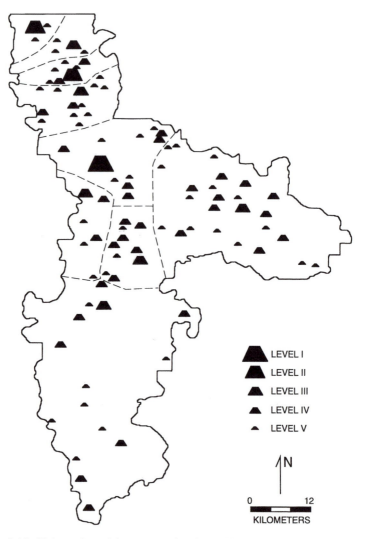

4.13 Civic-ceremonial centers and estimated boundaries of administrative districts, Late I.

of mounds. This difference may reflect a more regulated and formal ritual, governing, and military presence on the frontiers in contrast with the interior, where officials were likely more concerned with local agricultural production, market regulation, adjudication of disputes, and tax collection.

The trend toward an increased number of smaller administrative districts began with the partly autonomous valley arms of the Rosario phase, which were the political constituents of the new confederacy in Early I. But as Monte Albán's importance grew, territories in each valley arm lost autonomy and became subordinate administrative units of the new government. By Late I two of the valley arms were no longer single organizational units; rather, each was divided into three or four smaller territories of roughly similar size, each with its own leading and subordinate civic-ceremonial centers. As an experiment, we drew territorial lines splitting the distance between the large Late I centers and found that these hypothetical borders usually fell on topographic divides and in less densely populated areas. Also, both on these dividing lines and on the outer edges of the territories (toward the mountains), the lower-level civic-ceremonial centers usually had the closed, formal mound arrangements that we associate with border situations.

This analysis of the architecture and its distribution in the landscape involved recording the field measurements of mounds of all eleven phases of Oaxaca's archaeological sequence, estimating the period of construction of each mound from the sherds in the construction fill, calculating the volumes of construction for thousands of mounds, extracting and studying the sample of the best-dated mounds, creating typologies, drawing architectural plans for each site and plotting these plans on a large map of the valley to look for spatial patterns, testing hypotheses against the data, and rechecking and correcting errors. The pottery, stone artifacts, associations between settlements and land types, etc., all required similar list making, pondering, rechecking, and testing of alternative ideas. Recognizing possible patterns and evaluating what they might mean in terms of social change is one of the joys of archaeology, but between the discovery of sites in the field and their interpretation lie years of coding, list making, and analysis such as this. The difficulties of doing research in a region with a past as rich and complex as that of the Valley of Oaxaca has left us with a deep respect for its ancient inhabitants.

The hierarchy of status and wealth

Archaeology offers good perspectives on the wealth and status of individuals and households through the study of burial treatments, house forms,

and the distribution of artifacts of different types. But systematic evaluation of these variables requires representative samples – adequate
numbers of excavated houses from all wealth levels, from urban and rural
contexts, and from the different arms of the valley. Archaeologists in
Oaxaca do not yet have samples representative of the range of wealth
differences for any period. It is as if we were trying to estimate the number
of each size-class of fish in the ocean by using a hook and line from a
single boat. Nevertheless, for the data in hand from the Valley of Oaxaca,
when we "count fish" we do seem to find that the Rosario-phase fish were
about the same size, except for a few big ones, whereas by Late I we count
more big, medium-sized, and little fish. The status and wealth hierarchy
seems to have diversified and expanded.

A new practice that was established during the Rosario phase is represented by only one known example from that time: burial in specially constructed multichambered stone-lined tombs (Marcus and Flannery
1996:133). By Late I the range of funerary situations was quite broad,
from stone slab-lined tombs through formal burials in pits with offerings
of pottery to burials unaccompanied by offerings (see, e.g., Caso, Bernal,
and Acosta 1967; Marcus and Flannery 1996:ch. 12). Even the smallest
villages had some comparatively wealthy burials (Whalen 1981:90–103).

These burial data indicate increasing wealth and status for some households and individuals. Our regional survey also found, as early as Late I,
preliminary evidence for what may have been exceptionally low wealth
and prestige. Some outlying communities and some neighborhoods of
larger towns seem to have had only the minimum set of possessions, at
least so far as we can judge from surface remains (Kowalewski and
Finsten 1983). We do not know whether the artifact collections represent
systematic poverty or just relatively short-term occupations (longer
habitation would mean more refuse and more chance for discard of fancy
goods). Initial impressions seem to show that the transition from ranked
society to a more class-stratified society in which some households lacked
access to widespread elements of material culture occurred during the
Rosario-to-Period I time span.

Agricultural intensification and its consequences

Early and Middle Formative agriculture

Throughout the Early and Middle Formative, the total population of the
Valley of Oaxaca was far smaller than the potential population that could
have been supported in the region through maize farming (see Feinman
and Nicholas 1987; 1990b; Kowalewski et al. 1989:ch. 3–6; Nicholas

1989; Nicholas et al. 1986). This pattern of relatively abundant resources holds even for the more densely occupied Etla arm of the valley. The demographic and settlement changes from phase to phase during the Early Formative were not simple or direct responses to variability or change in agricultural potential. Sites generally continued to be situated on low rises near good alluvial land. Although settlements, especially many newer ones, were not always on or near the best land, they were often situated in areas where small-scale irrigation could easily have been practiced. With low valleywide populations and most settlements situated near reliable water sources, agricultural risk was minimized.

As early as the San José phase, maize farmers in the Valley of Oaxaca supplemented water from rainfall with simple irrigation techniques (Flannery et al. 1967). Their repertoire included pot or well irrigation – a labor-intensive strategy that can be employed in many alluvial zones of the valley. One aspect of well irrigation is that it can be implemented by a single farmer or the members of one household. Early Oaxaca farmers also likely secured water by building modest check dams and small channels to divert water from seasonal runoffs and the temporary streams that run during the rainy season. These irrigation techniques also required no central management and little or no labor from outside the household. Neither large-scale irrigation systems nor massive networks of canals have been important during the long history of this region.

Agricultural change during Early I

The regional population increased dramatically with the foundation of the new capital, Monte Albán. As we have pointed out, the new capital grew more rapidly than any other valley settlement, quickly surpassing San José Mogote. The organization and support of such a large center posed many problems that had not been encountered before. The inhabitants of Monte Albán could not feed themselves using just the farmland immediately surrounding the site. Rather they relied in part, through tribute or exchange, on surplus maize produced by households and communities located in the surrounding central portion of the valley and beyond.

By Early I, there were more than 250 settlements in the valley, and the regional population burgeoned to nearly 15,000 (fig. 4.14). Yet, as was the case as early as the Early Formative, this growth was not evenly distributed across the region. Most of the increase outside the capital occurred within 18–20 kilometers of Monte Albán (about a day's walk), in the central area, southern Etla, and the northern Valle Grande. The influence of the new capital on its immediate surroundings is clear, as

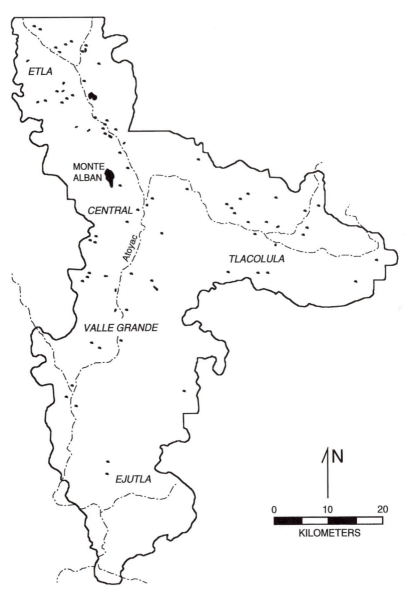

4.14 Early I settlement in the Oaxaca and Ejutla Valleys (sites with populations of twenty or more).

demographic growth was minimal beyond about 30 kilometers. Areas such as Guirún, Sola, and Ejutla still contained only a handful of sites, each less than 1 hectare in size. There are no known Early I settlements to the south of Ejutla in the Miahuatlán Valley and few if any in the mountains west of Etla and Monte Albán.

The impact of Monte Albán also is reflected in the environmental settings of communities. In Period I, many long-inhabited settlements continued to occupy the alluvium, as they had during the Early and Middle Formative periods. Beginning with Early I, however, there was a trend toward greater use of the agriculturally risky piedmont, where small, intermittent streams could be tapped for irrigation. With sufficient labor, this rolling terrain is capable of producing a considerable maize surplus in years of high rainfall, but there is also a significant risk of crop failure in dry years. In concert with population growth, this shift to more marginal piedmont settlement was most pronounced within 18–20 kilometers of the capital. Piedmont areas in the extreme southern arm of the valley remained virtually uninhabited. The heavier occupation of the piedmont near Monte Albán likely reflects the opportunity that these farmers had to market or barter their grain surpluses to the population of Monte Albán. At the same time, trade and other social mechanisms that linked Monte Albán to its surrounding settlements could have supplied a safety net for piedmont agriculturalists adversely affected by dry years. At greater distances from Monte Albán, piedmont and other farmers would have faced higher transport costs and had less access to the economic buffering provided by intraregional exchange networks made possible by this emergent form of regional integration.

Another development indicative of the agricultural consequences of the new regional organization is the region's first piedmont irrigation system, constructed during Early I on the lower slopes of Monte Albán. Even with the possibility of producing two or three crops a year, this canal system was not large enough to yield food for more than a fraction of the capital's population, but it is another example of Monte Albán's influence on changing agricultural strategies.

With a much larger regional population than in the Early and Middle Formative and therefore more agrarian labor, the valley's residents in Early I could have produced much more farm surplus than their predecessors. This surplus was necessary to support Monte Albán and its significant nonagricultural population. Locating more settlements in the piedmont zone near the capital was one way of generating this surplus, yet greater dependence on rainfall and water control led to an expanded risk of crop failure. The result was greater interdependence between Monte Albán and surrounding settlements than had existed previously between

San José Mogote and its smaller neighbors. Greater integration was required not only to move the necessary surplus to Monte Albán but also to provision areas experiencing crop failure. The denser occupation of the piedmont zone would not have been possible for long without this integration.

Agricultural change during Late I

Late I saw an intensification of many of the trends just described. The population of the capital continued to grow, tripling to more than 17,000. Residential construction covered much of the main hill at Monte Albán by the end of the phase, and sizable neighborhoods occupied adjoining hills. Population also continued to grow outside the capital. With about 750 settlements in the Valley of Oaxaca, the total population tripled to more than 55,000 (fig. 4.15). As in Early I, most of the growth (about 75 percent) occurred within 20 kilometers of Monte Albán, where the rate of expansion was even more rapid than at the urban center itself. The available alluvial land was more crowded, and there were not enough permanent tributary streams to provide each farmer with access to dependable sources of irrigation water. As a result, the expanding population in the area of the valley most directly influenced by Monte Albán spread into more and more marginal piedmont localities. At the same time, the largest tract of prime agricultural land, to the south in the Valle Grande, continued to experience relatively slow growth. Together these patterns of growth suggest that proximity to Monte Albán continued to be a key determinant of settlement location. The availability of prime farmland could not have been the sole factor in Late I settlement, as new villages were founded in the densely populated central area while relatively unoccupied blocks of good farmland remained elsewhere. Perhaps one of the most significant questions remaining is the relative role and importance of top-down elite coercion versus bottom-up household choices in these settlement decisions.

As before, because of temporal and spatial variations in rainfall, not all farmers in the piedmont areas would have been able to produce successful crops in any one year. As these same families concentrated on intensifying agricultural production, they would have had less time to practice other productive activities, regardless of whether their crops were successful. A more tightly integrated regional production and exchange system, accompanied by increases in the scale of craft production, may have been established in response. By the end of Late I, this intraregional exchange network likely included much of the valley, although economic interactions and interdependence were probably heaviest near the capital.

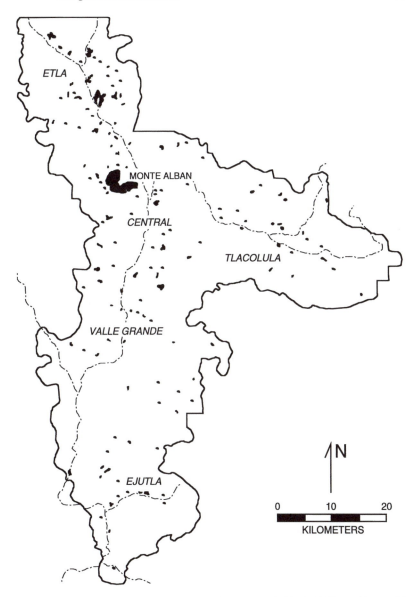

4.15 Late I settlement in the Oaxaca and Ejutla Valleys (sites with populations of fifty or more).

Another trend not seen in Early I was growth at the edges of the central valleys, especially in areas just beyond the physical boundaries of the Valley of Oaxaca proper, in Ejutla, Guirún, Miahuatlán, and Sola and, for the first time, in a very small way, in the mountains west of the valley. While the highest population growth rates for the Valley of Oaxaca were recorded for the Rosario/Early I transition, several of these outlying areas experienced their greatest growth spurts during the subsequent Early I/Late I transition, after Monte Albán was well established. Although some scholars may elect to see this dispersal to previously sparsely occupied areas as reflecting pressure on resources in more central parts of the valley, populations within the Valley of Oaxaca proper were still considerably below what agricultural resources could have supported. Instead, demographic growth in these more distant areas may have been spurred by the establishment of new macroregional exchange and interaction relationships that were formed with the emergence of the state.

Food exchange and domestic foodways

The establishment of Monte Albán in what formerly had been a sparsely occupied area at the hub of the Valley of Oaxaca was integral to a major episode of transition that affected almost all facets of life. Some of the most dramatic changes were economic, with major shifts in systems of production and exchange. Both the foundation of the city and the heavy occupation of the foothills surrounding it had significant economic consequences for households.

As we have seen, the utilization of the piedmont zone in the central area began early in Early I and intensified in Late I. Communities in these areas could produce bountiful crops when rains were abundant and timely, but buffering them in low-rainfall years would have required support networks that must have been in place by Period I. In contrast to alluvial farmers who could depend on well irrigation when rains were scarce or unusually late, many piedmont agriculturalists would have been entirely dependent on precipitation and the small-scale strategies of water divergence (e.g., check dams, small canals) to capture runoff from sporadic summer downpours. If the elite at Monte Albán wished to tap into the considerable agrarian surpluses that could be produced by the occupants of the piedmont settlements during wet years, they had to ensure that these communities could procure the necessary maize when their harvests were inadequate because of periodic droughts (Blanton, Kowalewski, Feinman, and Appel 1982:43–45).

The concentration of people at Monte Albán also had repercussions on systems of exchange and production. The residents of Monte Albán could not have fed themselves if they depended exclusively on farming lands within 2–4 kilometers of the site, yet it is unlikely that residents of Monte Albán ranged much farther to farm. Other valley communities occupied the terrain beyond 2–4 kilometers, and transport costs would have made the use of such lands at greater distances prohibitively costly for the residents of the capital. The small canal irrigation system on the slopes of Monte Albán would not have provided enough maize to feed the entire site population in dry years (O'Brien et al. 1982). These local food imbalances at Monte Albán perhaps would have been exacerbated if, as we expect, many of its residents were not farmers. Skeletal analyses show that the city's Period I inhabitants were reasonably healthy, and not severely malnourished or on the edge of starvation (Hodges 1989). These findings point to the existence of exchange links that generally brought sufficient food supplies to the city.

Both the more intensive settlement of the piedmont adjacent to the capital and the expansion of irrigation indicate that farmers living at and around Monte Albán intensified their production. Ceramic evidence derived from regional survey collections also supports this interpretation (Feinman 1980, 1986). Pottery, which first appears in the archaeological record shortly after 2000 B.C., was made primarily in a variety of bowl and jar forms prior to Period I (see, e.g., Flannery and Marcus 1994; Payne 1994). The most common shapes included large cooking jars, smaller water jars, neckless jars (*tecomates*), flat-bottomed bowls, rounded-bottom bowls, and cylinders. In Period I this formal diversity increased (Blanton, Kowalewski, Feinman, and Appel 1982: appendix 7; Caso, Bernal, and Acosta 1967; Kowalewski, Spencer, and Redmond 1978; Kowalewski et al. 1989:appendix 6), with new shapes including the tortilla griddle or comal (Feinman 1986; Feinman, Blanton, Kowalewski 1984; Winter 1984) (fig. 4.16).

Maize had been an important food in Oaxaca since before the advent of sedentary life (ca. 1500 B.C.). Early Oaxacans most likely ate maize in a variety of ways (Flannery 1976), including roasted, as gruel (*atole*), and probably as tortillas, but there was no specific utensil for heating tortillas before Period I. The advent of the comal may not signal the first tortillas, but it probably does indicate that tortillas were becoming a more significant part of the diet. Their expanding role provides clues to key shifts in Oaxacan lifeways during Period I (Blanton, Kowalewski, Feinman, and Finsten 1993:75). Tortillas require significant effort to prepare, especially grinding the corn and forming the flat pancakes, and they do not store well. Unlike *atole* or roasted maize, they travel well and can easily be consumed away from home without requiring heavy ceramic vessels for transporting and heating them. Thus, while the daily

4.16 Man selling comals on market day at Ayoquesco de Aldama in the southern part of the Valley of Oaxaca.

production of tortillas required the investment of more household time and labor, the consumption of tortillas may have facilitated work both farther away and for longer durations.

In our surveys, we found that Period I comals were most abundant in the area immediately surrounding Monte Albán (Feinman 1986). They were rare at sites located near the edges of the valley. The distribution of comals conforms to the assessments from settlement and land-use analyses that suggest that agricultural production was more intensive close to the regional capital and that the increased production brought with it changes in household economy and technology.

Craft production

The intensification of agrarian production had consequences for household labor allocations. More time spent in the fields intensifying agricultural output or in the kitchen preparing labor-intensive foods such as tortillas meant that individuals had less time to perform other necessary domestic tasks. Adjustments clearly had to be made in household time budgets, and one aspect of household behavioral change was in non-agricultural production.

Since the Early Formative a small minority of households in the Valley of Oaxaca had produced goods for exchange (Pires-Ferreira 1975, 1976). House excavations in several Early and Middle Formative communities indicate that this "specialized" production for exchange principally involved 1) exotic raw materials (such as marine shell) that were fashioned into ornaments (see fig. 1.4 for examples), or 2) local products that were destined in part for distant localities; one local material, magnetite, was worked into polished mirrors. In Oaxaca, most of these specialized products were used as adornments or grave goods and were largely consumed by wealthier households. Much of this specialized production was carried out by households in San José Mogote, although such activities were not limited to that early center. For example, certain households in the smaller village of Tierras Largas may have worked macaw feathers (Winter 1972).

Some Early and Middle Formative households may have engaged in the specialized manufacture of such utilitarian goods as pottery and chipped stone tools (Flannery 1976; Flannery and Marcus 1994:ch. 15), but many households appear to have produced these essential items for themselves. Salt is one basic good that may have been produced only by certain communities, since it often was procured from natural springs, which have a limited distribution (Drennan 1976:ch. 7).

By Period I, specialized craft production seems to have become more common, also occurring at higher intensities and volumes (Feinman 1980, 1986; Feinman, Blanton, and Kowalewski 1984). Predictably, evidence for this activity is most apparent in the vicinity of Monte Albán, where household labor allocations were most affected by shifts in agricultural strategies. Many agricultural households in this sector of the valley may have been less able to find the time to make their own stone tools or fabricate their pots and thus increasingly depended on specialist production. Nevertheless, at least some sites with evidence for high-volume ceramic manufacturing have been found in all arms of the valley. By Late I the most common bowl forms were more homogeneous across the region and were produced using more standardized methods. These shifts were associated with the increasing prevalence of characteristics reflecting concern for ease of manufacture and transportability: simplification and replication in decorative design, elimination of appliqué and supports, stackability, and increasing use of more uniform clays and higher firing temperatures (fig. 4.17). Fired clay molds were used for the first time. In concert, these changes point to more specialized ceramic manufacturing than in prior phases; the Late I potters were

4.17 Late I pottery, illustrating simplification, elimination of appliqué and supports, and stackability. Redrawn from Caso, Bernal, and Acosta (1967: fig. 175).

making larger volumes of basic ceramic goods for exchange, and this craft activity played a more central economic role in their households. There is still no evidence that this specialized production at high intensities was occurring anywhere outside domestic contexts (Feinman 1986).

At present, there is less direct evidence for the specialized manufacture of craft goods other than pottery in Period I. The contents of an excavated pit on the Main Plaza at Monte Albán has revealed that onyx may have been processed into ornaments in quantities beyond the requirements of a single household (Winter 1984). We suspect that chipped and ground stone tools, lime plaster, and other goods were being produced by specialized craft workers, especially at settlements in the central area, but additional findings are needed to confirm this interpretation. Nevertheless, specialized ceramic manufacture, a key industry in Oaxaca as elsewhere in Mesoamerica, clearly was more prevalent in Period I than it had been earlier. In conjunction with the great growth at Monte Albán and the heavy occupation of the piedmont, it seems clear that the intensity of local exchange networks had increased by this time.

Systems of exchange

During the Early and Middle Formative, most communities, even San José Mogote, could feed themselves using lands immediately surrounding their settlements (Nicholas 1989). Likewise, most households could produce most (although not all) of the goods that they needed for everyday life. Most if not all houses had exterior subterranean pits in which surplus agricultural produce could be stored (Winter 1976). Oaxacan households produced certain goods for exchange, but often these goods (made by specialists) incorporated exotic materials or were made in part for export outside the valley (Pires-Ferreira 1975, 1976). Many of these exchanged goods were relatively rare. Obsidian, shell, stingray spines, and pottery from other areas of Mesoamerica were among the items traded into the Valley of Oaxaca, but these too were not exchanged in large quantities (Pires-Ferreira 1975). The items that moved across regional boundaries often carried important information and conveyed symbolically significant messages, but the archaeological record indicates that they were comparatively few.

We know relatively little about the social means of exchange that moved goods among households, settlements, or regions. Because the volume of exchange was low, we suspect that many goods were moved through reciprocal exchanges, including gift exchanges between relatives, neighbors, or exchange partners, and barter (similar to the exchange behaviors discussed in Humphrey and Hugh-Jones 1992). Certain goods may have been cycled during communal feasts or redistributed through leaders and chiefs. No centralized storage facility associated with the central control of food or the caching of large amounts of portable wealth has been found, suggesting that the exchange system was not centered around or organized by a chief.

With the shifts in production strategies and the growth in population during Period I, the volume of intraregional exchange undoubtedly increased (Feinman 1991). No longer could much of this exchange have been handled primarily through reciprocal gift exchanges. In theory, centralized redistribution by the emergent authorities at Monte Albán could have handled large volumes of goods but this is unlikely. The hilltop location of the capital would have required movements of significant quantities of goods up and down the hill. Furthermore, we lack any indication of grain and other storage features on the scale required for a large redistributive economy. We also have no evidence that any production took place in nondomestic, state-supervised workshops; rather craft manufacture appears to have remained in residential contexts. Instead of a redistributive economy, we postulate that much Period I exchange occurred in marketplaces frequented by household producers and consumers (Blanton 1983; Blanton, Kowalewski, Feinman, and Appel 1982:65–68; Feinman, Blanton, and Kowalewski 1984). If production was primarily in the hands of households, it is hard to see how distribution or exchange could have been controlled by a central political institution. Market exchange and marketplaces certainly were important when the Spanish first described sixteenth-century Oaxaca, and they continue to be important institutions to this day (Beals 1975; Cook and Diskin 1976). It seems reasonable to suggest that these thriving contact-period institutions had a long prior history, even though it is difficult to identify market exchange or even marketplaces archaeologically. We still lack indisputable evidence for this hypothesis. Our surveys did find at least one site that had features consistent with a marketplace – a low hill in the middle of the Valle Grande area, south of Monte Albán, not in one of the district capitals or other civic-ceremonial centers, but between them, at the intersection of three proposed district boundaries. The site dates to Early and Late I. It has no mounds; instead it has a large (55 by 38 meters), open, easily accessible platform bordered by large boulders. There is an unusual amount of artifactual evidence here for specialized production: misfired pottery, dense concentrations of chipped chert and quartzite, a tunnel into bedrock apparently to mine quartz, two circular bedrock features that may have served in a grinding or pounding operation, and a bark beater for making paper (Blanton, Kowalewski, Feinman, and Appel 1982:262). The location, open plaza, and artifactual evidence are what one might expect for a market.

By Period I, Valley of Oaxaca communities were much more economically interdependent than ever before. The intensities at which some craft producers manufactured their wares greatly exceeded the past. A wide range of diverse goods were being produced and consumed. In sum, with the establishment of Monte Albán, it is clear that the volume and nature of production and exchange were markedly different from what came before.

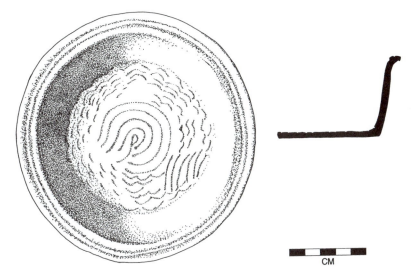

4.18 Late I-type G-12 bowl. Redrawn from Caso, Bernal, and Acosta (1967: fig. 130).

Art, ideology, and ritual

The evolution of ceramic forms and designs

A major change from the San José phase to Period I was in iconography and decorative elements on ceramic objects. The prominent Early Formative design motifs had been the fire-serpent and earthquake, stylized representations of supernatural forces that we have linked to the dual social organization of San José Mogote and its dependent communities. Rosario-phase serving bowls, by contrast, often had more abstract geometric designs (see, e.g., Drennan 1976:40–1). There are a few plates with modeled frog or other animal effigy, but these occur infrequently. Fire-serpent and earthquake motifs declined in the Rosario phase, and they were gone (or turned into unrecognizably abstract standardized grooves along the inside of the vessel rim) by Period I (Drennan 1976:56–65)(fig. 4.18). Most decorated Rosario-phase vessels were manufactured in a fancy burnished gray ware, a ceramic category that became more frequent and widespread in Period I (Drennan 1976:56).

Many Rosario-phase households had plain hourglass-shaped charcoal braziers. The late-Rosario elite residence at San José Mogote described earlier had an anthropomorphic incense brazier of a type that became

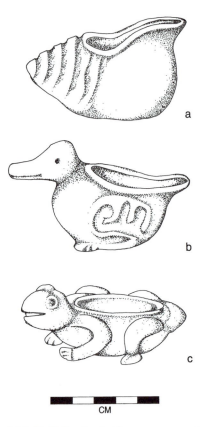

4.19 Early I animal effigy pots: *a*, seashell pot; *b*, duck pot; *c*, toad pot. Redrawn from Caso, Bernal, and Acosta (1967: figs. 104, 102, 110).

more frequent in later periods. Human figurines were fairly common during the Rosario phase, as in earlier Formative phases and were often explicitly female, perhaps even representations of real people. Similar figurines continued into Period I, although in reduced frequencies. Clearly the Rosario phase was transitional, carrying forward some features of the Early and Middle Formative pottery motifs and forms while presaging changes to come.

During Early I, the pace of change in ceramic design quickened. The variety of forms and decorative motifs increased, and skilled potters turned out more fancy pots in many forms, including seashells, ducks, shoes, turkeys, toads, and rabbits. Plates took the form of frogs and fish, these last complete with scales, fins, and puckered lips (figs. 4.19 and 4.20). They made jars bearing effigies of Cocijo, the Zapotec representa-

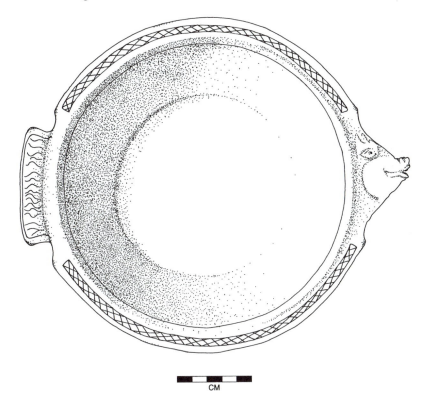

4.20 Period I fish plate. Redrawn from Paddock (1966: pl. 9).

tion of lightning-clouds-rain, which often accompanied burials in tombs (see, e.g., Whalen 1981:ch. 6). Frying-pan-shaped incense burners had handles in the forms of earth monsters and snakes (Caso, Bernal, and Acosta 1967:146–74).

Temples in Period I civic-ceremonial centers in the Valley of Oaxaca and at Monte Negro, in the mountains 65 kilometers northwest of Monte Albán, had a new form of brazier (Acosta and Romero 1992; Caso and Bernal 1952) – a cylinder featuring a man's face with a down-turned mouth (in Mesoamerican art usually representing a feline). The mouth is open and the eyes perforated so that in the dark the glowing coals would have made the brazier look like an eerie jack-o'-lantern. The figures had headdresses, each one slightly different but all with a version of glyph C (for Cocijo) and often a leaf or a cob of maize growing out of a vessel of water.

Jars and cups for holding, pouring, and drinking liquids were much

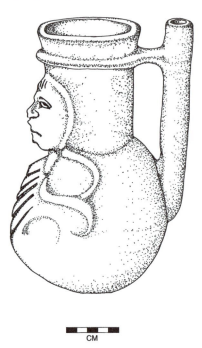

CM

4.21 Late I bridge-spout vessel. Redrawn from Caso and Bernal (1965: fig. 2).

more common than in the Rosario phase, perhaps indicating a greater need for specialized vessels for ritual feasting. Although the excavated sample size is small, the numbers of vessels for holding liquids that are found in burials are quite striking. At the small village of Fábrica San José, the Rosario- and earlier Guadalupe-phase burials were typically accompanied by only a few pots, most of which were serving bowls (Drennan 1976). The burials from Period I and later also had serving bowls, but additionally they included many tall, cylindrical vessels and bottles with tall, narrow necks and tall spouts attached to the vessel with a "bridge" of clay. These bridge-spout vessels are a hallmark of burial ritual beginning in Late I (fig. 4.21). A single Late I burial from Santo Domingo Tomaltepec had twenty-one bridge-spout and similar bottles (Whalen 1981:90–95). The number of pots in this offering is as impressive as any yet known from Monte Albán. Santo Domingo Tomaltepec at the time was a hamlet of fewer than one hundred inhabitants, at the bottom of the population-size hierarchy and in the lowest rank of the civic-ceremonial hierarchy. Apparently elaborate burials were not limited to large centers such as Monte Albán. As at Fábrica San José, the pre-Monte Albán I burials that had pottery offerings tended to have just a few each, typically the same forms used for everyday cooking and serving. Four Period I tombs excavated at Yagul, which at the time was a fifth-rank village 35 kilometers east of Monte Albán in the Tlacolula Valley, also had many vessels for liquids and a brazier with Cocijo elements similar to the braziers described above from Monte Albán (Chadwick 1966).

At Monte Albán too, burial rituals seem to have involved many containers for liquids, including large and miniature cups, vases, bridge-spout vessels, and bottles, in addition to narrow-necked jars with Cocijo or anthropomorphic faces, seashell pots, and pots with representations of ducks, turkeys, frogs, toads, and fish (Caso, Bernal, and Acosta 1967). Most of these occur in burials and tombs, but occasionally they have been found in offerings apart from funerary contexts.

We interpret the alterations made in Period I ceramic artifacts as indicating several concurrent aspects of social and cultural change. For one, the more widespread occurrence of a greater array of forms suggests not only a growing dependence on specialized producers but also increased consumption of a wider range of high-quality ceramic artifacts by many households. Although by Late I the fine gray wares had become formally and decoratively simpler and showed more evidence of mass production, these decorated wares were available to a wide range of households and constitute the most frequently occurring diagnostic pottery on virtually all sites of the period. The increasing frequency of vessels that may have been used in ritual feasting reflects the rise of a new religious and ritual system and also may hint at a growing affluence in which many households certified social status through feasting behaviors that necessitated new categories of decorated pottery vessels.

Inferring ideology from ceramic artifacts

In native Oaxacan mythology people were given agriculture through a continually renewed covenant: the earth provided rain (since clouds come from earth), and in return people had to make sacrifices. We suggest that as part of its state-building strategy the governing elite of the region appropriated the ancient symbols of this covenant – the Cocijo symbols so prominent in the pottery of Monte Albán and elsewhere in the valley (fig. 4.22) – and made them part of the ideology of the Monte Albán state.

The Cocijo cult was a universalizing ideology that was not particular to a single place, dynasty, or segment of society. The cult was based on older, widely shared beliefs, but in Period I Cocijo was magnified into the most important supernatural force. His cult subsumed the earlier symbolism of

4.22 Classic-period representation of Cocijo on a funerary urn excavated from a tomb below a residential complex in Ejutla, Oaxaca.

fire-serpent and earthquake under a unifying concept of fertility and renewal. The Cocijo cult was about rain and fertility of the earth. The fish, amphibians, birds, and other animals modeled on pots were representations of the cult. The men whose faces appear on temple braziers adorned themselves with Cocijo symbols. The jars, cups, and vases containing liquids represented rain as did the blood gushing from the torture victims on the Main Plaza.

In indigenous Oaxacan folk religion today, sacrificing and praying for rain renews a covenant, an agreement between a person representing a family group and the supernatural forces (Monaghan 1990). With the growth of the Valley of Oaxaca state of Period I, Cocijo imagery was promoted at all levels of society, from households in smaller communities to the most important rituals carried out in the temples and in the houses of powerful families at the most important centers, including Monte Albán. The construction of a more hierarchically complex society in the Valley of Oaxaca cannot be disentangled from ideological and ritual change. The evolution of lightning-clouds-rain imagery and ritual was as much a part of the evolution of culture and society as were the expanding hierarchy of settlements, the intensification of agriculture, and the increasing specialization of craft production.

State formation from the perspective of the household

One of the major advantages of a regional perspective is that it allows the assessment of the consequences of social change in a wide range of social settings. Research in the major civic-ceremonial centers provides invaluable information about the evolution of political institutions, but we want to understand more about society in a broad sense to contextualize the political change. Here we look at what happened to households during the course of the extraordinary changes that occurred in the Valley of Oaxaca during Period I. Our perspective is enhanced by combining data gained from excavations of houses (see Drennan 1976; Flannery 1976; Marcus and Flannery 1996; Whalen 1981; Winter 1972, 1974) with the findings of our regional settlement pattern survey.

We have noted the central importance of regional unification, centered at Monte Albán, in the political evolution of Period I. What is most striking, however, is that this political realignment brought in its wake a substantial transformation of society, culture, and technology that affected every household to at least some degree, although generally households more distant from the new capital were less affected. We are not sure to what degree other episodes of state formation in other world areas were accompanied by such a thoroughgoing transformation of society and culture. In most areas of the world the data that would allow this kind of comparative assessment are lacking. Other cases of state formation may have been unaccompanied by such a pronounced systemwide transformation. For example, we cannot detect very much change in ordinary households and their technology during the periods following primary state formation in Early Dynastic China (e.g., Chang 1986:364), but, again, this impression may be a product of insufficient data. At any rate, the Valley of Oaxaca might not be a typical example of state formation and social transformation.

We have already documented many of the ways in which households were affected by the growth of the state. For one, families had an increased propensity to migrate to cities and other new communities in the central area of the valley and elsewehere. Some probably came to the valley from other regions. Fertility increased, fueling the formation of many new households and rapid overall population growth. Exactly how fertility increased is not known. Since the same food crops, agricultural technology, and health conditions had been in place for a thousand years, fertility probably did not suddenly increase in Period I due to a new nutritional or health factor. If leaders saw political and economic advantages in a larger population, they may have promoted a pronatalist ideology to encourage growth (Blanton, Finsten, Kowalewski, and Feinman 1996:32). Another plausible hypothesis is that new demands for labor and new economic opportunities created conditions favoring a more rapid formation of new households. Parents could have increased the working capacity of their households by having more children. Or a younger age at marriage would have increased the rate of household formation and led to greater fertility as women began having children earlier.

In addition to these demographic shifts, households increasingly made their livelihoods by means of a diverse array of occupations and productive strategies. Particularly within a 30–kilometer radius of the capital, virtually every household reoriented its economic strategies. Many of the households of the capital (in addition to a smaller number in lower-ranking centers) probably were not engaged in farming as virtually all households had been in prior periods. Since Monte Albán's population represented about a third of the region's total throughout Period I, at least several hundred households were not fully agricultural in Early I; this figure increased to thousands of households during Late I. In both phases, certain households in secondary centers probably also were not entirely engaged in farming. By comparison, probably less than a hundred households were involved in part-time production of exotic goods during the San José phase. Also during Period I, an increasing number of rural households became more specialized in nonagricultural production, of which pottery making is the most obvious. Farming households intensified production, often in the marginal environments of the piedmont.

Did the combination of political change, migration, increased fertility, occupational change, and agricultural intensification result in benefits to many households, or did the growth of the state benefit primarily a few powerful households living in the major centers? The answer to this is important, because differing theories of state formation posit different outcomes in people's material conditions of life. In the Valley of Oaxaca, various kinds of evidence all point to the same conclusion: Overall, although the osteological data indicate few changes in mortality and morbidity, there was evidently a substantial increase in material consumption for most households during Period I. This is not, however, to say that state expansion always brings material improvement, in Oaxaca or elsewhere; during Periods IIIA (A.D. 300–500) and IIIB (A.D. 500–700), it was accompanied by a declining rural standard of living (Kowalewski et al. 1989: ch. 8 and 9), and even by Late I we have detected some comparatively poor households in the valley. Yet, from our vantage, it appears that during the initial phase of state growth in the Valley of Oaxaca, material life improved for most households.

We have already proposed that the formal and decorative elaboration of pottery, especially the burnished grayware complex, with its vessel forms specialized for ritual feasting, provides evidence of increasing elaboration in the world of goods during Period I. Perhaps an even better indicator of increasing consumption can be seen in changes in house construction (see box 7 in chapter 3). In particular, the broad transition to mud brick in domestic construction indicates a "great rebuilding" in some ways comparable to that in England between 1570 and 1640 (Brunskill 1987:27). There, as in Period I Oaxaca, for the first time most households could afford houses built of relatively expensive materials. Mud brick is a superior construction material in terms of both durability and protection from weather extremes; to this day in the Valley of Oaxaca it is preferred over wattle and daub in spite of its higher initial cost.

In addition to these construction advantages, we propose that mud brick may have had symbolic significance for Period I households; its only prior use had been in public buildings (going back to the San José phase) and in a few elite houses, such as the "chief's house" of Rosario-phase San José Mogote (Marcus and Flannery 1996:109, 131). Although there were differences between ordinary and elite houses in Period I (the latter were more frequently elevated on platforms and more often had enclosed patios) (e.g., Whalen 1981:90–95), status distinctions nevertheless were comparatively blurred because houses of all levels in society made use of the same basic construction materials.

Change after Period I

Period I was the first of a series of three major growth episodes in the valley's pre-Hispanic history; population growth and rapid social change occurred again during Periods IIIA (A.D. 300–500) and V (A.D. 1000–1520). The valleywide growth that characterized Period I was not sustained during the subsequent period. During Period II (100 B.C.–A.D. 300) the region's population declined by 19 percent, to around 45,000 (Kowalewski et al. 1989:ch. 7), and some of the greatest losses were in the central area, the adjacent Etla arm to the north, and the northern Valle Grande – areas that had experienced much of the growth during Late I. The capital also experienced a 16 percent decline, to less than 15,000. One possible explanation is that forest clearing and farming in the piedmont immediately surrounding Monte Albán prompted environmental degradation in that rather delicate zone, which in turn led to community abandonments and population losses. However, Ejutla, far removed from the central hub of the valley, experienced an even greater decline, losing more than a third of its population. Late I Ejutla Valley sites had generally been located near some of the best land in that region, so it is difficult to use the same explanation to account for its decline.

Another plausible explanation for the demographic decline is that during Period II Monte Albán turned more of its attention to the conquest of other regions (Redmond 1983; Spencer 1982). As the state embarked on significant imperial ventures, including conquest and tribute exaction outside the Valley of Oaxaca, there may have been less pressure on households to increase their production. For example, fewer Period II communities were located in the agriculturally risky piedmont zone near the urban center. At the same time, other parts of the central valleys, especially Tlacolula and the adjacent Guirún area, experienced population growth. Other people may have moved out of the valley as neighboring areas were colonized. An emphasis on imperial ventures outside the valley and less meddling by the elite in internal affairs could have had demographic effects, bringing about a reversal of Period I's growth.

5   Synthesis and conclusions

In the last chapter, we looked at the implications of a new political order in the Valley of Oaxaca, drawing on findings from regional archaeological surveys, site excavations, and the interpretation of carved stone monuments. We now step back and consider this historical sequence from a more theoretical and comparative perspective. How does the ancient Oaxacan case relate to what we know about other early states and their development?

First, Period I in the Valley of Oaxaca was one of the world's relatively few instances of primary state formation. No other states existed, so far as we know, at this time elsewhere in Mesoamerica. Period I is therefore of considerable theoretical importance for understanding the process of state formation in general. How and why do people construct states when they lack any model or prior knowledge of similar political systems? What form will this new type of government take, what functions will it exercise, and how can it become widely accepted in society as a legitimate power? We try to understand what factors led to the eventual enactment of a new political course for the region.

We need not assume that the early state in Oaxaca was entirely a planned phenomenon. Many of the processes involved were probably responses to unanticipated events, and it is unlikely that there was a unanimity of opinion about the nature of the new political system or even whether there should be one. Separate factions probably had differing views of the ideal nature of government, and some probably resisted the development of a state. For example, some elite factions of the Rosario-phase chiefdoms may have opposed the new arrangement, which represented a loss of autonomy. We are not yet in a position to understand in detail the historical events surrounding what may have been a controversial social process, but fine-grained, problem-oriented archaeological research eventually will provide a more complete picture. Even now, we have substantial information pertinent to understanding political change, enough to allow us to apply what we know of the Oaxaca experience to a critical evaluation of theories of state formation.

Monte Albán and the traditional theories of state formation

Political scientists define the state as a specialized and hierarchically organized political system exercising sovereign, legitimate authority within a defined territory. Everybody in the world today lives under the authority of a state. Anthropologists can point out that this was not always so. There was a time 6,000 years ago – not so long ago in the total time of human history – when there were no states. From the third millennium B.C. until the twentieth century, some people lived under the authority of states while others did not. Overall, most societies in the experience of our species did not have the state. People made decisions by consensus; they thought about social relations as social networks or groups of kin instead of people as subjects of a government, and the boundaries of societies were often loose or overlapping. These were the bands and tribes of hunter-gatherer, pastoral, and horticultural people. In chiefdoms, hereditary heads of polities often had great authority in certain matters, but they lacked the minions of officeholders that give the state its greater clout; the authority of chiefs was more fleeting and less pervasive. The governing apparatus of chiefdoms also was less costly to society. Many philosophers and social scientists have asked: What brings about state formation?

The real question is: If *Homo sapiens* lived well for so long without the state, then why did it develop? Since we know from many historical sources that the state can be an instrument of oppression, expropriation, and legalized brutality, it is worth reviewing a selection of answers to this question that have been proposed by social philosophers and social scientists in our Western tradition. As we review these ideas, we address whether any of them might be relevant to the experience of the Valley of Oaxaca just after 500 B.C. We add a few of our own ideas, based on what we have learned from research in Oaxaca. Among the approaches that have been used to understand state formation are diffusion, conflict theory, cultural ecology, and functionalism.

Diffusion

According to diffusion theory, the state arose in one place, for whatever reason, and then spread to other societies. Around the turn of the twentieth century, diffusionists were active, tracing the worldwide distribution of culture traits. Egypt often was regarded as the ultimate source of many culture traits found around the world. The development of complex New World societies, in particular, has frequently been attributed to influence from the Old World, from, variously, Egypt, the Phoenicians, and the Lost

Tribes of Israel, among a host of others (see, e.g., Feder 1996). Such ideas have been repeated in the contemporary popular literature, on television, and in movies, so they strike a chord with many people despite (or perhaps sometimes because of) the implicit racism of the assumption that Native Americans could not build complex societies on their own (Bernal 1980).

The main problem with the diffusionist explanation is that it is contrary to the facts. Nowhere in the world can the earliest states be shown to have come about by simple diffusion from a single source. Later expansion into peripheral areas did spread state institutions, but early states simply did not have the power to impose complex state organization on distant populations. In Asia, horses and war chariots made conquest at a distance logistically possible, but this was after 2000 B.C., more than 1,000 years after the first states of Mesopotamia and Egypt. We can document a vast middle Old World zone of ancient social interaction extending from Egypt to China (Hall 1997) – for example, domesticates such as wheat, sheep, goats, pigs, and cattle eventually became widespread over this area – but archaeologists generally agree that within this broad interactive domain there were at least four instances of primary state formation, each with its locally distinctive characteristics. These primary developments occurred in the Nile Valley, in Lower Mesopotamia, in the Indus Valley, and in North China (Service 1975). The New World states that developed in Mesoamerica and the Central Andes were clearly distinct from the Old World states and from each other. Diffusion does not help us understand why the state developed during Period I in Oaxaca.

Conflict theory

Conflict theorists tend to view human societies as inherently contentious, rife with struggles between economic classes, political factions, and ethnic or other social groups. For these scholars the state is an institution that can reduce conflict, for example, by limiting feuding and warfare; hence the state is a product of conflict. The most frequently expressed theory of this type is one originally published by Frederick Engels in 1884, on the basis of his reading of some of Karl Marx's ideas (Leacock 1972). In Marx and Engels's scenario, increased economic activity brings in its wake a process of social class formation that divides society between those who control resources and those who do not. The ensuing class-based conflict necessitates the development of an institution – the state – that can contain conflict while protecting the property interests of the economically dominant class. Thus Marx and Engels's state was the despotic instrument by which the ruling class retained control of the means of production and suppressed the lower classes. Another version of conflict theory points to the necessity of a social contract. According to Thomas Hobbes, we have the state, despotic as it is, because life under it is more orderly and civilized than it was before the state developed (Service 1975:ch. 2). Of course, anthropologists can show that life in stateless societies was not always anarchic or savage (Service 1975:ch. 3).

Several findings of Valley of Oaxaca archaeological research suggest the importance of conflict in state formation, but we doubt that they support the idea of state formation due to conflict alone. Although there is evidence going back to the San José phase of economic differentiation between households, we are unable to document distinct economic classes and class-based conflict prior to Period I, if then. There is, however, evidence that conflict of some kind did increase just prior to the founding of Monte Albán. A warfare-sacrifice complex indicated by the *danzantes* monuments began during the Rosario phase and was elaborated at Monte Albán. This complex evolved at the same time as an intensifying competition between discrete polities within the valley and perhaps with polities beyond. Thus competition, in the form of warfare between discrete polities, rather than internal class conflict, may be one causal factor in the political changes leading to state formation.

Did the Monte Albán state develop to contain this interpolity competition? Our data suggest a decline in Valley of Oaxaca warfare in conjunction with the development of the Monte Albán state. Surface evidence of burned houses (pieces of burned daub or other burned materials) occurs less frequently in Period I than earlier (Kowalewski et al. 1989:116). We infer from this finding that the new state institution had the ability to reduce the frequency of warfare between the separate Rosario-phase polities and perhaps raiding by outsiders. But from this conclusion we certainly do not mean to imply that state formation was necessarily an entirely peaceful process. As we have said previously, it is likely that Monte Albán struggled during Period I against internal or subregional opposition to its fledgling authority, but our data are not sufficiently fine-grained to provide a detailed picture of these crucial early years.

Cultural ecology

A cultural-ecological perspective overlaps with conflict theory in some features, but rather than seeing state formation as an outcome of conflict between social groups, cultural ecologists see it as a product of adaptation to aspects of the natural environment (Sanders and Nichols 1988). Normally, this adaptive process is set in motion by "population pressure," defined as population growth to levels beyond what can be supported with a given suite of domesticated plants and animals, natural resources, and agricultural technologies (Sanders and Price 1968). Population pressure leads to conflict over desired agricultural resources and eventual domination by those groups who are better able to achieve control of them. In one version of this scenario, agricultural intensification, which also is seen as a response to population pressure, is central. In agricultural intensification more and more labor and technology are applied to smaller and smaller areas of land to keep up with increasing demands for food (Boserup 1985). The state is the institution by which increasingly powerful rulers control the valuable, scarce agricultural resources or the labor of farmers.

In the so-called irrigation theories first elaborated by Karl Wittfogel (1957), agricultural intensification involved water management for swamp drainage, flood control, and large-scale irrigation. Such water control necessitated a more centralized political organization to build and manage facilities and to allocate this key resource (Adams 1966:ch. 2). The organizational complexity that developed in the context of water management then was transferred to other organizational spheres and became the basis for the centralized political forms of the state.

It is no coincidence that the major Old World primary states developed along the courses of major rivers – the Nile, the Tigris and Euphrates, the Indus, and the Huang Ho (Yellow). In all of these river drainages, water control can substantially increase yields, and all of them did eventually see the construction of major water control systems. Even though we do not always know the exact relationship between organization for water management and primary state formation, this is all very suggestive. The water-management variant of cultural-ecological theory was worth looking into, and archaeologists have expended substantial effort studying the evolution of such technologies (e.g., Adams and Nissen 1972). However, in Mesoamerica, there is no close association between major river systems and early states. The major rivers – the Balsas, the Papaloapan, and the Coatzacoalcos – were not sites of early state formation. The Valley of Oaxaca's river system is of comparatively small scale (a person can easily walk across the Atoyac during most months of the year), and we have little archaeological evidence for the large-scale water management that so impressed Wittfogel in his studies of Chinese history. Archaeological surveys do point to small-scale canal irrigation in the piedmont, but this occurred after the establishment of Monte Albán. That canal irrigation in the valley was more a consequence than a cause of political change suggests a more complex process than the simple cause and effect chain of events posited by traditional cultural-ecological theory (Wright 1986).

Like conflict theory, cultural-ecological theory seems able, in part, to provide a useful explanatory framework for the Valley of Oaxaca. To apply it to Oaxaca, however, requires that we amend some of its central ideas in several ways. All too often, archaeologists with no better explanation use population pressure as a deus ex machina (literally a "god from a machine") – in drama this is a highly improbable device used to get out of a difficult situation in the plot. But what makes populations grow? Why does population grow in certain places at specific times?

Regional archaeological surveys reveal many cases in which population grew very slowly or not at all during the time leading up to state formation (Wright and Johnson 1975). This was the case in the Valley of Oaxaca (Feinman et al. 1985; Nicholas 1989). In Mesopotamia as well as in Oaxaca at the time the first states were formed, populations were well below the levels that theoretically could have been supported given the existing agricultural resources, farming risk, and technology. Good land and water resources were not in short supply, even during Period I, and there is no evidence of direct Monte Albán administrative control over water, land, or production. The new capital seems to have been intentionally placed away from the region's most valuable land.

Theorists who espouse demographic pressure consider population as constantly growing. The only true variable is the local environment; therefore one is left with an awkward kind of environmental determinism. Yet Mesoamerica, China, Peru, and Europe each contain a wide variety of climatic, soil, and vegetational zones, and the state emerged in each of these extremely diverse natural settings.

More holistic, multivariate explanations should take account of human agency, the social environment, and the ways in which people create and are shaped by cultural and social factors as well as the natural environment. Our model for the rise of the Monte Albán state includes population growth as an important consequence (not an initial cause) of the political and economic changes that began around 500 B.C. These changes include both agricultural intensification and the farming of extensive new lands using already known technology, such as irrigation, as people worked to meet the requirements of the new, larger urban capital. Compared to San José Mogote, the support of Monte Albán demanded more work, more time, and more agricultural returns from households. We see population growth and agricultural intensification as consequences of this greater demand (and reward) for labor.

An important dimension of population growth and agricultural intensification is not that they caused state formation, but that they may have produced sociocultural stresses that required an elaboration of governing institutions, including the Monte Albán state. In this scenario, causality is circular (or mutual-causal) rather than linear. A "kick" to the system (the founding of Monte Albán) brought about intensification and population growth, and these processes, in turn, increased the demand for a more hierarchical form of governance.

We can benefit from ethnographic studies of piedmont canal irrigation systems similar to the ones that were first built during Period I to illustrate what might have been involved in these mutual-causal interactions (Hunt and Hunt 1974; Lees 1973). These present-day irrigation systems are small and do not require a centralized state for their construction or maintenance. Tasks can be handled by community-level cooperative organizations. But in dry years, when the need for irrigation water is greater than the supply, these small water management systems may collapse, crippled by conflict that the local governing institution cannot manage. In these circumstances, today, officials of the Mexican government step in to restore order and keep production going. During Period I, the occasional need for irrigation management at this level was likely an unintended outcome of intensification, one that required a nascent governing institution to develop the ability to cope with just this kind of drought-induced social stress. And with the rapid population growth of Period I, the frequency and intensity of such conflicts over water (and probably other disputes about land and even arguments between sellers and buyers in the markets) would have increased, placing ever greater demands on political authorities if they were to maintain an acceptable level of agricultural production.

We have already mentioned that, following Monte Albán's founding, many households moved to the piedmont, thereby exposing themselves to higher levels of agricultural risk in dry years. This population movement would have forced Monte Albán to expand its governing activities to include the transfer of surpluses from storage or surplus areas to deficit areas – a process that would have required logistic coordination, access to labor, and a degree of legitimization that would allow the state also to appropriate surpluses to cover the administrative costs required to manage a regional-scale economic system.

It is obvious from this discussion that some of the key interactions relating to political change, including population growth, agricultural intensification, and an increased use of marginal environments, are variables pointed to by cultural-ecological theories. Growth of the Monte Albán state was indeed importantly conditioned by demographic and environmental factors that cannot be ignored. However, state formation in the Valley of Oaxaca was not principally the environmental adaptive process that cultural ecologists would consider it. We know that social change was not driven by population pressure alone but was the outcome of a process involving complex causal interactions among a number of variables, including environment, agriculture, and population. Many other factors, however, must be figured into the causal equation.

Functionalism

The cultural-ecological and conflict theories see the state as primarily a despotic institution that evolved to protect the interests of the wealthy and landed or to control labor for warfare and agricultural intensification. Materially, some sectors of the despotically governed society are expected to suffer, be they an economic underclass or marginalized groups lacking access to prime agricultural resources. By contrast, functionalists argue that no despotic state could be sustained for very long, since the great majority of people simply would not agree to support it. From a functionalist perspective despotism would be dysfunctional (Service 1975:303). Instead, successful, enduring states would have to provide services to the population as a whole. Functionalist arguments come in two major varieties, economic and communications.

According to Service, an emergent centralized governing institution serves to redistribute goods between households of production specialists, thus providing greater overall access to a wide range of goods produced across an environmentally diverse region (Service 1975:ch. 17). Service was influenced by the economic historian Karl Polanyi (Dalton 1968), who proposed that the major economic system of an early state would be the government itself, as a redistributor of goods, rather than a commercial market system or interpersonal (gift) exchanges. Polanyi doubted that market systems had developed prior to the modern world's capitalist economies.

Recent research on chiefdoms and early states largely has discredited economic functionalist theory, at least the extreme forms of it that follow Polanyi (see, e.g., Brumfiel and Earle 1987; Earle 1978; Feinman and Neitzel 1984). There is great variability cross-culturally and over time in the degree to which early states engaged in redistribution. Probably the foremost example of a redistributive system was the Inca empire. There, archaeologists and ethnohistorians have documented the capacious storage facilities, state production enterprises, and redistributive rituals that linked households tightly to the state economy (Murra 1980).

In contrast, redistribution was not carried out on such a significant scale in ancient Mesoamerica. Instead, what we know from early Spanish descriptions indicates that Mesoamerica was characterized by well-developed markets that served as society's major conduits of exchange and specialized production (Berdan 1975). Nowhere in Mesoamerica do we find storage features on the scale of those in Inca administrative centers. Placed high above the valley floor, Monte Albán is not optimally situated to serve as a major economic node in its region. We have few indications of large-scale production or storage either there or in secondary centers dating to Period I.

The Monte Albán state apparently did, however, play a key economic role in its region, and its growth apparently did provide material benefits for many households. Yet, in spite of this seeming support of the functionalist theory, we cannot accept it without modification. The Monte Albán state was not primarily a redistributive institution. Its economic role was substantial but more subtle and indirect than functionalist theory would predict. With the growth of the state, the region became more highly integrated, with a larger percentage of households settled in marginal piedmont environments where they needed to be linked to a larger economic system that could reduce agricultural risk. The evidence for greater specialized production implies increased frequency of exchange in specialist-produced goods between households. There are indications of an overall increase in economic activity, from agriculture to craft goods, and in the labor devoted to the construction of mud-brick houses.

Given the absence of centralized storage facilities, it is likely that much of the increased economic activity in Period I was mediated by the growth of a market system rather than by a highly developed state redistributive system. Unfortunately, our data are not fully adequate to allow us to assess the amount of commercial activity that took place. Even if market transactions were important conduits for goods, however, there still would have been some state involvement. For one thing, the greater regional integration provided by the new political system would have made it possible for people to move about safely in what had previously been a much more segmented, contested social landscape. And we know from comparative studies of pre-Hispanic market systems in Mesoamerica and peasant market systems elsewhere that these systems require some kind of adjudicative authority to weed out fraud and punish wrongdoers and to ensure the safety of marketplaces and transport routes. Economic development would have created an additional arena in which state authorities would have been expected to provide administrative services, adding to the state's workload as the Period I system increased in scale, integration, and complexity.

The second variant of functionalist theory views the state primarily as an information-processing system. According to this communications functionalism (see, e.g., Johnson 1987), as a society becomes larger in scale and more complex it tends to generate more information. To maintain optimal social functioning, governmental institutions must develop greater capacity to gather, transmit, and process information. This increased capacity is accomplished in part by adding levels of administrative hierarchy to the governing institution. Higher levels are charged with the coordination and monitoring of lower ones (Flannery 1972).

To what extent was the early Monte Albán state an information-processing institution? It was a political and a religious hierarchy, certainly. The number of civic-ceremonial centers increased over time, and no matter how one counts the levels it is clear that the hierarchy of centers expanded and assumed new functions. This hierarchy continued to grow throughout Period I. The architecture of the state, in the form of closed mound groups and plazas, reached down the hierarchy and out to the margins of the region. This hierarchical growth is one of the most striking indicators of the growth of the state in Period I. But what did the officials of centers at different levels in the hierarchy actually do? If they handled information, of what kinds was it? The archaeological evidence is thin. No particular realm of social life seems to be emphasized: for example, there are no large storage facilities like the Inca's, no written records of economic transactions as in ancient Mesopotamia, and no written accounts of priestly rituals as in Early Dynastic China. Centers in the regional hierarchy have temples and public plazas suited for ritual events along with the residences of the elite who probably were officials in the state hierarchy (though there have been few excavations to document the latter). Perhaps local officials collected tribute and made sure that Monte Albán was supplied with labor, food, drink, baskets, pots, mats, lime plaster, cement, and other necessary items. Perhaps they were concerned with land tenure, water rights, public order, the functioning of the market, and assembling warriors. They may have resolved disputes. Local officials with priestly roles may have carried out rituals of the Cocijo cult. All of these activities, of course, involved gathering and processing information, which required a hierarchy of offices. But communications functionalism is too limited because the state clearly did more than just process information. It also was involved in politics, warfare, and legitimizing itself. Nothing in the material record of the valley indicates an information-processing crisis that preceded and then was resolved by state formation.

New theoretical directions

Of the major theories of state formation just outlined, we find only the diffusionist approach to be of little value. None of the other theories can fully explain what is known about the Monte Albán state, yet elements of each of their predictions are consistent with the facts of Period I political change. Our foray into traditional theory illustrates the value of a multi-variate, mutual-causal approach over adherence to the more traditional ones that rely on single variable, linear causal frameworks. At the same time, the study of state formation in Oaxaca points us in new directions. One of the new frameworks that we think is important focuses on the interactions of a regional polity, such as the Valley of Oaxaca, with other regional systems and even with Mesoamerican civilization as a whole. The adoption of an interregional perspective highlights the evolutionary variable we have called boundedness. What is the role of governing institutions in the management of exchanges across a region's borders? Can changes in the way in which a region is bounded induce evolution in its governing institutions? We address these questions in the following section by contextualizing the growth of the Monte Albán state in its larger setting.

Changing interregional linkages

There is relatively little indication that the people of the Valley of Oaxaca defended or monitored the physiographic boundaries of their region before 700 B.C. Archaeological surveys conducted in these outlying upland areas have found almost no settlements earlier than this; even the subsidiary valleys that border the Valley of Oaxaca, like Ejutla, Sola, and the Guirún area, were extremely sparsely settled. The agriculturally risky mountain zones that surround the valley may have been undesirable places in which to live. In the Valley of Oaxaca itself, most early settlement was situated in the Etla arm near the head town of San José Mogote. Few communities were located close to the edge of the valley, and none were placed in clearly defensible settings or in locations allowing them to control interregional movement. The region's boundaries, we infer, were open and permeable.

Across Mesoamerica, the period between 1200 and 900 B.C. was marked by social change related to the development of the Early Horizon interaction sphere (see Grove 1997 for a recent review). In many regions, including the Valley of Oaxaca, the Basin of Mexico, the Gulf Coast, the Pacific Coast of Chiapas, and highland Morelos, head towns emerged and monumental constructions were raised. These monuments differed in kind as well as in building material. For example, earthen mounds and large carved basalt heads were erected at some Gulf Coast sites, and platforms of stone masonry and squared adobe were built at select settlements in the Valley of Oaxaca.

Increasingly more formal and institutionalized patterns of leadership and social inequality seem to have developed after 1200 B.C. Certain households may have been in contact with each other through the exchange of ritual goods and elaborate adornments. Marine and freshwater shells, jade, metallic ore mirrors, obsidian, turtle shell, and highly decorated pottery moved across physiographic boundaries through trade and gift giving. A set of decorative motifs including the were-jaguar and the fire-serpent was widely shared across much of Mesoamerica, although societies had their own artistic conventions for representing them. Early Formative Mesoamerica was not dominated by any single region. Rather, the whole region was a network of autonomous polities in which emergent leaders and perhaps others exchanged goods, and likely mates, across considerable distances.

After 700 B.C., the nature of interregional linkages began to shift. We see indications of this shift in the Valley of Oaxaca, with significant changes in the Rosario-phase and Period I settlement patterns. Although the Rosario-phase population of 2,000 remained roughly comparable to what it had been earlier, settlements were now placed closer to the edge of the valley. One of these perimeter settlements was positioned defensively on a natural spur in low piedmont near a pass above Mazaltepec in western Etla that serves as a gateway to the west and the Mixteca Alta. This settlement was protected by hills on all sides except to the east, where it was fortified by a double wall of large stone blocks. This revetment was erected sometime between the Rosario phase and Late I, the only phases in which this spur was inhabited. This site may have been one of the first fortified sites in the Valley of Oaxaca, and its location suggests that it functioned to control or monitor the region's boundary at a crucial point of entry.

Several other Rosario-phase centers in the Valley of Oaxaca also were strategically located, and the number of such places increased in Period I. In Etla, the town of Huitzo was located in the foothills at the northern end of the valley. In the Valle Grande to the south, the towns of Tlapacoyan and Tilcajete were both situated near key passes that link the heart of the valley with areas beyond. At the frontiers of the Valley of Oaxaca, populations remained extremely sparse, but the earliest village in the Guirún region was established during the Rosario phase at the edge of a natural corridor called the Hormiga Colorada (Feinman and Nicholas 1996). A few new settlements were formed to the south in the Ejutla Valley. At greater distances, the numbers of people in areas such as the Cuicatlán Cañada, Huamelulpan, Tehuacán, Tamazulapan, and Nochixtlán were increasing at this time (Balkansky 1998; Byland 1980; MacNeish et al. 1972; Redmond 1983; Spores 1972; Winter 1989).

Elsewhere in Mesoamerica, more areas were occupied by chiefdoms and ranked societies than ever before, and the geopolitical map was becoming increasingly complicated. To monitor what was happening and to compete with other elites on this scale required considerable time, effort, and followers. Leaders at San José Mogote would have had to face potential competitors at other Valley of Oaxaca centers, as well as a more complex Mesoamerican political environment. Centers such as Chalcatzingo in Morelos and La Venta on the Gulf Coast, which had been key places in their respective regions for centuries, lost population and importance (e.g., Grove 1987:440–41). At the same time, Izapa on the Pacific Coast of Chiapas and Cuicuilco in the Basin of Mexico grew in size and monumentality (Lowe, Lee, and Martínez Espinosa 1982). From the Mixteca Alta of Oaxaca to the Maya region from two to ten travel days away, significant political shifts were taking place. The population of the Valley of Oaxaca, at the center of Mesoamerica, had to adjust and respond to these changes.

Archaeological knowledge of the era between 700 and 300 B.C. is spotty, but a brief review of the Mesoamerican landscape suggests that it was a time of dramatic population growth, political development, agricultural intensification, and perhaps increased military concern (Carmona Macías 1989; Manzanilla and López Luján1994; Weaver 1993). In the Basin of Mexico, the first ceremonial construction occurred at Cuicuilco; this site appears to have been the largest center in the basin at that time (see Sanders, Parsons, and Santley 1979:76–77; Vaillant 1931). There were, however, at least five other head towns in the region (Sanders, Parsons, and Santley 1979:97–98). William Sanders and Jeffrey Parsons, who surveyed most of the Basin of Mexico, describe this time period as one of rapid population growth (Sanders, Parsons, and Santley 1979:97–98). People were making greater use of irrigable land, signaling agricultural intensification. Both the rapid population growth and agrarian expansion may have been related to increasing political competition, which may have triggered greater demands on households for followers, labor, and production.

In Puebla and Tlaxcala, the Texoloc phase (800–400/300 B.C.) was characterized by a doubling of the region's population, the initial development of towns (some with as many as 2,000 people), and agricultural intensification (terraces, irrigation canals, and dams) (García Cook 1981). Some of the larger settlements were positioned defensibly. Carved stone monuments that emphasized new calendrical and cosmological themes, including supernaturals associated with fire (Huehueteotl) and rain (Tlaloc), were erected. Large polychrome effigy censers representing Huehueteotl were used in ritual. Comals were employed as they were in Oaxaca, indicating a change in household food preparation and labor organization. In the Tehuacán Valley of Puebla, this time period was marked by a doubling or tripling of the regional population, with a concomitant increase in the number of sites, the site hierarchy, and civic-ceremonial construction (MacNeish et al. 1972). Quachilco, the region's head town, rose to prominence shortly after 500 B.C. (Drennan 1978, 1979). During these four or five centuries, the huge Purrón dam, also in the Tehuacán Valley, was enlarged significantly (Spencer 1993).

In the Mixteca Alta, northwest of the Valley of Oaxaca, head towns were established at Etlatongo in the Nochixtlán Valley (Zárate 1987) and Santa Cruz Tayata in the Huamelulpan Valley (Balkansky 1998). The growth of these towns coincided with sustained regional population growth. Shortly after 500 B.C. even larger centers were founded across the area. At one of these, Huamelulpan, carved stones that included Zapotec glyphs, albeit different from those in the Valley of Oaxaca, were erected (Gaxiola González 1984). The borrowing of the Zapotec writing system reflects a significant degree of communication, at least among elites. Many of these somewhat later centers were in defensible places (see, e.g., Acosta and Romero 1992).

After 500 B.C. the key Gulf Coast Olmec centers, San Lorenzo and La Venta, were eclipsed by new or expanded occupations at Tres Zapotes, Cerro de las Mesas, and El Trapiche (Coe 1965a and b; Drucker 1943a and b; 1953; Drucker, Heizer, and Squier 1959; García Payon 1965; Stark 1991; Stirling 1965; Weiant 1943). In the Tuxtlas, sizable increases in population were noted between 1000 and 400 B.C. (Santley and Arnold 1996) and marked demographic nucleation and hierarchy formation immediately thereafter. On the Isthmus of Tehuantepec during the period between 800 and 400 B.C. the key settlement of Laguna Zope grew to 90 hectares (with a population estimated at 2,000) (R. Zeitlin 1978, 1993). This site was one of the largest in Mesoamerica at this time and apparently had exchange and communication links to the north, east, and south.

On the Chiapas coast, east of Tehuantepec, a linear arrangement of mounds, plazas, and enclosures was constructed at Middle Preclassic Tzutzuculi between 650 and 450 B.C. (McDonald 1983). Down the coast at Izapa, the Escalón phase (650–450 B.C.) was the first period of widespread, intensive occupation (Lowe, Lee, and Martínez Espinosa 1982). The site continued to expand in the subsequent Frontera phase (450–300 B.C.) when stone monument carving also was begun. This latter phase was marked by the building of platforms and pyramids across central and western Chiapas. To the west in the uplands at Chiapa de Corzo (Lee 1969), raised-platform construction began in the Escalera phase (650–450 B.C.) with marked population growth during the following Francesa phase (450–300 B.C.). Ceramic spear points, of more symbolic than tactical value, were included in Francesa-phase burials, perhaps signaling an increasing concern with military matters; the burial assemblages from this phase also show more grave-to-grave distinctions, likely revealing increased degrees of social differentiation (Lee 1969). Farther south down the coast in the Escuintla region of Guatemala, a series of six 20–50 hectare centers, each with significant concentrations of monumental construction, were recorded (Bove 1989; see also Pye and Demarest 1991).

In the Maya Lowlands to the east, the period from 800 to 400 B.C. was a time of widespread village formation and rapid population growth (Sharer 1994). Large public platforms were built at several sites, including Altar de Sacrificios and Cuello (the latter in distant Belize). Toward the end of this period, significant growth and construction occurred at Nakbe and El Mirador in the Petén (Forsyth 1989; Sharer 1994). At Nakbe, a massive basal platform and a series of tall structures (one possibly 18 meters high) were erected between 500 and 400 B.C. (Sharer 1994).

The macroregional wave of political change during this era evoked responses in all regions, but the outcomes were not identical. The Valley of Oaxaca was at the geographic center of a changing world. To the north and west – in the Basin of Mexico, Puebla-Tlaxcala, Tehuacán, and the Mixteca – new centers with civic-ceremonial constructions were established. The rise of Quachilco in Tehuacán may have been particularly relevant for the populace of nearby Oaxaca. Major changes also took place along the Gulf Coast, and important new centers were established to the south and east – in Tehuantepec, Chiapas, and the Petén. The large Laguna Zope site, like Quachilco, was a perceivable threat that was less that one week of travel away.

Military symbolism evident at Chiapa de Corzo and Huamelulpan provides a strong indication that offense and defense were sufficiently real concerns to be incorporated into ritual contexts. In addition, we see the first use of writing and textual evidence for the Mesoamerican calendar at this time. New systems of information storage and display were devised and communicated. These changes include the *danzantes* complex in the Valley of Oaxaca. The symbolic system of were-jaguars and fire-serpents that had linked populations across much of this world was in decline, and in diplomatic and military matters new mechanisms for interregional competition were being tried out.

In some respects, the rise of Monte Albán in the Valley of Oaxaca may have been precocious in its timing and particularly dramatic in its militaristic epigraphy. Monte Albán was rather nucleated and urbanized compared with centers in other regions. In part, this may have something to do with the size and productivity of the valley as well as its geographically central position. The Valley of Oaxaca is larger and has more demographic potential than other valleys of southern Mexico, and it is more easily bounded and controlled from a single point than the Basin of Mexico, the Petén, or the Gulf Coast. At 500 B.C. it lay at the center of a network of new competitors. Monte Albán was one outcome of a Mesoamerican world undergoing a rather tumultuous transition.

The evolution of a core-periphery system

As in the small valleys of the Mixteca Alta, the regions directly surrounding the Valley of Oaxaca also experienced growth and sometimes their earliest permanent communities during this era. In the Guirún region, the first village was settled after 700 B.C., but a marked expansion took place after 300 B.C. In the long-occupied Ejutla Valley, rapid growth occurred between 500 and 200 B.C. The first village in the Sola Valley dates to roughly 500–300 B.C., but many more and larger communities were inhabited a century later. Similarly, the mountain region just north of the Valley of Oaxaca was permanently inhabited only after 500 B.C. (Drennan 1989), while the Peñoles region was settled after 300 B.C. (when twelve to fifteen settlements were established) (Finsten 1996). The small populations of these outlying areas could not have been the main threat to the peoples of the Valley of Oaxaca before the foundation of Monte Albán. As we have seen, such perceived challenges likely came from farther afield. Yet the rapid growth of these boundary regions corresponds in time with the emergence of a more unified valley population and a regional capital.

Intensified production and higher volumes of exchange have been documented in various Mesoamerican regions after 700 B.C. (e.g., Schortman and Urban 1991; Wonderley 1991), and these changes may have made the settlement of relatively marginal zones such as the mountains surrounding the Valley of Oaxaca more feasible. At the same time, the maintenance of these ties as well as defensive considerations had further implications for political authorities in the Valley of Oaxaca and elsewhere.

We are far from a satisfactory understanding of how and to what degree the Monte Albán state interacted with the developing polities and growing populations outside the valley (e.g., Joyce and Winter 1996). Our discovery of a category of centers that evidently served as boundary sites suggests a growing concern with boundary maintenance beginning during the Rosario phase and extending through Period I (Elam 1989). These sites suggest that interregional interaction was an important concern for the emerging polity, but we need more information about this domain of social action. We know from the presence of defensive features that offense-defense was a key activity, but did boundary sites such as Mazaltepec also regulate the flows of commodities and people? How did these centers figure in the scheme of regional governance? Was the emergent state able to monopolize interregional flows? To what extent did outlying areas become incorporated into a core-periphery system?

In our discussion of the powerful core states of A.D. 1500, we noted the presence of various kinds of fortified sites along the edges of empires and in conquered districts through which core-periphery interactions were managed (Smith 1996b). The boundary sites of Rosario through Period I, although smaller in scale than analogous features of the Aztec empire, may have served similar functions. They illustrate an important process integral to state formation, namely, an intensification of core-periphery interactions. Most sociocultural evolutionary theory emphasizes causal processes that took place within local cultural and environmental settings, including such factors as the growth of hereditary inequality, class conflict, population pressure, irrigation management, and economic redistribution. Although the evaluation of these theories has stimulated much useful region-focused archaeological research over the past five decades, new research strategies are needed if we are to arrive at a fuller understanding not only of state formation but also of the larger question of the role of core-periphery interactions in the rise of civilizations.

Additional theoretical issues

In discussing the growth of the Monte Albán state, we have pointed to increasing hierarchical complexity indicated by the growth of important centers and the social differentiation between wealthier and poorer households that is seen in the comparative elaborateness of burial goods accompanying the dead. However, it is not easy to understand precisely how this hierarchically constructed society was governed or by whom. Obviously, powerful authorities at Monte Albán could collect taxes, wage wars, engage in diplomacy, erect carved stone monuments, construct public buildings, manage urban problems, appropriate surpluses from producer households, and adjudicate disputes. But who were these authorities and how did they come to positions of power? Were there rulers or a governing council? We are at a loss to specify the nature of government, in part because there has not been sufficient excavation of Period I public buildings and elite houses, but also because there is so little written evidence from the period that would allow us to infer how and by whom power was exercised. No definite Period I rulers were named or represented in portraiture, and no ruling dynasties were recorded. No massive public funerary monuments of rulers have been discovered in the hundred-year history of Oaxacan archaeology. Stone-lined tombs held elite individuals, but they occurred in domestic contexts, under the floors of houses; they were not built as public monuments reflecting the glory of individuals or of dynasties.

Understanding the role of religion and ritual in the process of state formation is also problematic in the Valley of Oaxaca. We think that the promulgation of the Cocijo cult helped to legitimate the new authority at Monte Albán and its appropriation of a portion of the surplus production of households, but how? This symbolic system was not used or controlled exclusively by the state and its ruling families and their temples; Cocijo rituals performed in the temples of the major civic-ceremonial centers and in their most important elite residences were similar to the domestic rites involving special pottery and Cocijo imagery of households and of temples in smaller communities. While the new ideological system no doubt played a role in the legitimation of a state political system, it did so in a way that reminded people of a commonality of interests between the different sectors of society.

If we compare these features of the Monte Albán state with those of other early states, we can detect a substantial degree of cross-cultural variation in how states were governed (Blanton, Feinman, Kowalewski, and Peregrine 1996). For example, we can point to a number of societies whose rulers were more publicly named and shown in portrait art, including some in pre-Hispanic Mesoamerica (the Olmec and the Classic Maya)(Gillespie 1993:73). In fact, this type of individual-oriented polity is for most people the prototypical early state. In ancient Egypt, for example, a king list goes back to nearly the fourth millennium B.C. and includes approximately 170 pharaohs over a period of 3,330 years (see, e.g., Strouhal 1992:267–68). The average reign in Egypt was about seventeen years. If the length of reigns was similar in the Valley of Oaxaca, we would expect twenty-three named rulers for the 400 years of Period I, but not one Oaxaca ruler is known with certainty. Later, during Period III, several Monte Albán rulers are named in public monuments in and around the Main Plaza, but they number only five during this 400-year period (Marcus 1980, 1983a and b).

More excavation has been carried out in the Main Plaza area of Monte Albán than in any other archaeological site in Oaxaca; therefore we doubt that the small number of ruler images found there can be attributed to a simple failure to locate them. We propose that the early Monte Albán system of governance was one that inhibited the public glorification of rulers. Oddly, elites in other centers in the valley and elsewhere in the southern highlands may have had more freedom to have their images carved in stone. As Caso (1965b:857–58) noted, "Monte Albán is not where the most beautiful sculptures of this period [IIIA] are found" (see, e.g., Marcus 1983c). This lack of portraiture provides evidence that public glorification of rulers was most inhibited at the very place where it would have really mattered: Monte Albán.

Pre-Hispanic Mesoamerica did have states that were in some ways comparable to ancient Egypt in that we have considerable historical information about rulers and their exploits. The Maya kingdoms of the Classic period (A.D. 300–900) are one example (Schele and Miller 1986). Because these Maya rulers depended on their extensive linkages across networks of states for marriages, exotic prestige goods signifying power and wealth, and military allies, we have come to refer to them as "network" polities (Blanton, Feinman, Kowalewski, and Peregrine 1996). Other Mesoamerican states, such as Period I Monte Albán and Teotihuacan from A.D. 300 to 700 (Pasztory 1997:ch. 8), were more "introverted" and less individualized, and it is difficult to identify particular rulers or to understand how power was exercised. We call states like Monte Albán of Period I and Teotihuacan "corporate" because their political structures were evidently less centered on particular ruling families and they placed greater emphasis on social and cultural integrative mechanisms in the construction of a complex polity (Blanton, Feinman, Kowalewski, and Peregrine 1996). Evolutionary anthropology's tendency to focus on political centralization and, in particular, the rise of ruler cults as the central fact of political evolution in early states has left us with insufficient conceptual tools for understanding these more corporate polities.

How to study early states

As we have seen, the emergence of the Monte Albán state marked an episode of dramatic transformation in the Valley of Oaxaca and the entire southern highlands. The shift from the Rosario phase to Period I was characterized by key transitions in demography, exchange, production, extraregional relations, symbolic systems, ritual, the natural environment, and political organization. Even the ways in which people prepared their food, built their houses, and buried their dead were significantly affected. In Oaxaca, these last centuries B.C. represent one of the four greatest episodes of transformation in the entire history of the valley, the others being the transition to sedentary village life (ca. 1500 B.C.), the sixteenth-century Spanish conquest, and the twentieth-century incorporation of the valley into the global economy of the modern world system.

The emergence of the Monte Albán state is a key hinge point in this region's past. The basic organizational structure established in Period I was retained and embellished by the Zapotec for at least 1,000 years, and certain cultural elements and traditions that we first see at this time have remained important in Oaxaca to this day (we review these in the Epilogue). If we are to explain and reconstruct the long-term history of the Oaxacan peoples, then we must understand the changes that reshaped their world around 500 B.C.

Monte Albán was perhaps the first city to emerge in Mesoamerica. As we have argued here, its rise was interwoven with dynamic political and demographic shifts that were taking place throughout Mesoamerica at the time. Because it was so precocious, the case of Monte Albán's emergence is important for the study of pre-Hispanic Mesoamerica and beyond. As anthropological archaeologists we are interested in unraveling the processes and events behind Monte Albán's development because each case of state formation has its own distinctive aspects. No state is typical, and the specific processes that gave rise to different states are generally rather variable. Since there is no single pathway or necessary sequence of events toward state development, it is important for archaeologists to collect information on as many of these historical processes as possible.

It is not clear whether the neoevolutionist's stages of sociocultural evolution (e.g., Service 1975) can be applied to the Valley of Oaxaca sequence. The San José phase, often thought to represent the chiefdom stage of a developmental sequence, does not appear to us to have all the requisite features of such a stage. We have interpreted the organizing structure of society as consisting of a moiety system and public ritual, rather than a chiefdom based on ranked descent groups. Wealth differences between households are evident in some aspects of material culture. So are individual status distinctions, some but not all of which may have been hereditary. There was widespread interaction and exchange involving exotic goods in which some households evidently participated more than others. But this is a long way from saying that political rule was in the hands of a hereditary elite – a chiefdom.

We suggest that the social changes evident during the San José phase cannot be considered the direct precursors of the state. Both the San José-phase moiety system and the pan-Mesoamerican international style were long gone by the time Monte Albán was founded, and the dual symbols of sky and earth had been transformed. None of these institutions figured into state formation at Monte Albán. Instead, the antecedent conditions for state formation appeared well after the San José phase, primarily during the Rosario phase. These conditions include the possible development of a chiefdom at San José Mogote and several other competing centers in the valley, the elaboration of a warfare-sacrifice complex, and the growth of centers and populations in areas adjacent to the valley and elsewhere in Mesoamerica that may have required the valley's leaders to pay more attention to boundary maintenance and military security.

In the sweeping evolutionary-stage typologies of neoevolutionist theory, world history goes from hunter-gatherers to tribes, chiefdoms, states, and perhaps capitalism. The stage typology makes it too easy to think in terms of one repetitive sequence of prototypical forms of societies and to neglect important aspects of variation in sequences and societal types. The study of state formation in the Valley of Oaxaca is of value both in itself and because its distinctiveness forces us to rethink our explanatory theories.

Epilogue

The masonry mud-brick house that first appeared in Oaxaca in Period I persists until this day, but it never completely displaced wattle-and-daub structures, which are used today for kitchens, bathrooms, or the first stages of long-term home improvement plans. Comals are still used to make tortillas, although today it is more common to buy machine-made tortillas. Burial in a family tomb under the house was favored until the Spanish priests and governors put an end to the practice in the sixteenth century. The Zapotec writing system also persisted – on human leg bones, stone monuments, and bark paper or deerskin – until the sixteenth century. Scholars know only parts of this record today, but some of the content and subject matter of the old writing system can be found in bits and pieces in the oral traditions of Zapotec-speaking villages.

The Cocijo cult became the artistic hallmark of the Zapotec in the Classic period, when it was closely associated with funerary rituals, especially at Monte Albán and the major secondary capitals of the state. The funerary urn, an elaborate confection of baked mold-made clay pieces, garishly painted, is the signature art object of the period, and many of these funerary urns wear the accoutrements of Cocijo. After the collapse of the Monte Albán state, the big urns were no longer made and Cocijo retreated to the realm of the clouds and the esoteric prayers of local priests and the tenders of pilgrimage shrines.

Clay figurines became even more popular in the Classic period than they had been in Monte Albán I, but these figurines were mass-produced, mold-made representations of a small set of human and animal motifs, a far cry from the individualistic females of the Formative. After the Classic period, clay figurines almost disappeared.

Anyone who thinks that human technology naturally progresses will be convinced otherwise by the course of Oaxaca's pottery making. In Monte Albán Early I specialist potters made rather fancy, well-made serving bowls. Bowls were simplified in Late I, and then in Monte Albán II became more elaborate again, now decorated with flanges, mammiform supports, and bright red and orange colors. The pottery of the Classic period, in contrast, is the plainest, drabbest, least decorated, most mass-produced, and most standardized of the entire pre-Hispanic sequence (and, by the way, the most distinctively Oaxacan). Perhaps this pottery was the functional and stylistic equivalent of our plain white disposable paper plate. By the Postclassic period, however, potters were again turning out more varied, hard-fired, and well-burnished decorated wares, sometimes with polychrome painted designs.

San José Mogote, once the leading town in the Valley of Oaxaca, had its moments of glory and demise. In Period I, of course, the capital and all its public functions moved to Monte Albán, and San José Mogote may or may not have had as many inhabitants as it had in the Rosario phase. But in Period II, it underwent a huge construction boom. A ball court was constructed for the Oaxacan form of the Mesoamerican ballgame, and a great plaza was laid out like the Main Plaza at Monte Albán. After Period II San José Mogote was never again a major center, although some people always lived there. Today it is a village of 1,000 people. The earthen mounds where ancient buildings were erected are still visible, and the town supports an excellent museum displaying the artifacts from the excavations.

Monte Albán grew to a population of around 25,000 in the Classic period. The ruins of the Main Plaza and residential terraces are still very impressive and accessible to visitors. Today the capital of Oaxaca, Oaxaca de Juárez, is not on the mountaintop, but in the center of the valley, across the river from the ancient capital, and has nearly half a million inhabitants. The ruins of Monte Albán are under considerable threat. The growth of the modern city, commercial tourism, unwise use of the site, recent house construction, and all the products of contemporary development exert pressures from all sides. It remains to be seen whether it will receive the continued serious study and enduring preservation that its past importance and majesty suggest it richly deserves.

Bibliographical essay

CHAPTER 1

In his *Origins of the state and civilization* (1975), Elman Service developed a comparative framework that has influenced most subsequent research including our own. While there has been an abundance of work completed since the publication of Service's book, it stands as a useful starting point for inquiry; no recent work has attempted such a broad synthesis. Many summary sources describe Mesoamerican civilization and its development. Coe (1994) is a readable introduction, as is Weaver (1993). Blanton, Kowalewski, Feinman, and Finsten (1993) compare and contrast patterns of change in three of Mesoamerica's most influential regions, the Basin of Mexico, the Valley of Oaxaca, and the Lowland Maya. The massive *Handbook of Middle American Indians*, published by the University of Texas Press in 16 volumes from 1964 to 1976 (and in two supplementary volumes in 1981 and 1984) provides a broad overview of Mesoamerican peoples and cultures from the earliest foragers to societies of the twentieth century. A recent work on the Late Postclassic, emphasizing Aztec society and its empire, is Smith (1996a). He integrates ethnohistoric and early colonial sources with the growing body of archaeological data from this period. Berdan et al. (1996) provide a massive compendium of information on the Aztec empire. The book's authors analyze these data from economic, political, and ideological perspectives. The chapters in Sharer and Grove (1989) discuss the Early Horizon and its features in various Mesoamerican regions.

CHAPTER 2

Marcus and Flannery (1996) provide a detailed, but highly readable account of the Valley of Oaxaca's environment and its social evolution leading up to Monte Albán. Here they effectively combine their excavated data from sites such as San José Mogote with some aspects of our settlement pattern data. Earlier but still useful sources on the Valley of Oaxaca include Flannery, ed. (1976) and Flannery and Marcus, eds. (1983). We summarize the results of our archaeological survey of the Valley of Oaxaca in Blanton, Kowalewski, Feinman, and Finsten (1993:ch. 3). The chapters in Price and Feinman (1995) assess current thinking about the nature and causes of social inequality in societies similar to those of Formative Oaxaca.

CHAPTER 3

The main source for Monte Albán's origin and growth is Blanton (1978). Monte Albán's foundation as an example of synoecism was proposed in the same work. This idea is also discussed in Marcus and Flannery (1996:ch.11).

CHAPTER 4

The major sources for our discussion of the Period I transformation are Blanton (1978), Blanton, Kowalewski, Feinman and Appel (1982), and Kowalewski et al. (1989). The results of settlement pattern research reported in these sources are augmented by data from several excavation projects, especially Michael Whalen's at Santo Domingo Tomaltepec (Whalen 1981, 1988), Robert Drennan's at Fábrica San José (Drennan 1976), and Marcus Winter's at Monte Albán (Winter 1974). Our discussion of change in the Period I pottery depends heavily on Caso, Bernal, and Acosta (1967), who report on the pottery they discovered in the course of excavations at Monte Albán.

CHAPTER 5

Authors writing about social evolution typically present, and defend, some particular theoretical orientation. A conflict emphasis stemming from Marx's and Engels's ideas is found in Haas (1982) and Fried (1967). Cultural ecological causality is promoted in Sanders and Price (1968) and in Johnson and Earle (1987). Service (1975) favors an economic functionalist approach, while Wright and Johnson (1975), Johnson (1987), and Flannery (1972) elaborate on a communications functionalist argument. In our opinion, none of these approaches has adequately dealt with the problem of cross-cultural and temporal variation in early states (Blanton, Feinman, Kowalewski, and Peregrine 1996); this issue is also addressed in several of the chapters in Marcus and Feinman (1998). Also lacking in this literature is any adequate treatment of how early states are embedded in larger interactive systems of world-system scale. Sources like Blanton, Kowalewski, Feinman, and Finsten (1993), Hall and Chase-Dunn (1993) and Schortman and Urban (1992) urge us to adopt more geographically inclusive research strategies.

Bibliography

Abu-Lughod, Janet L. 1989. *Before European hegemony: the world system, A.D. 1250–1350*. Oxford: Oxford University Press.

Acosta, Jorge R. 1965. Preclassic and Classic architecture of Oaxaca. In *Handbook of Middle American Indians*, vol. 3, pt. 2, ed. Gordon R. Willey, pp. 814–36. Austin: University of Texas Press.

Acosta, Jorge R., and Javier Romero. 1992. *Exploraciones en Monte Negro, Oaxaca: 1937–38, 1938–39 y 1939–40*, ed. José Luis Ramírez and Lorena Mirambell Silva. México, D.F: Instituto Nacional de Antropología e Historia.

Adams, Robert McC. 1966. *The evolution of urban society: early Mesopotamia and pre-Hispanic Mexico*. Chicago: Aldine Atherton.

1974. Anthropological perspectives on ancient trade. *Current Anthropology* 15:239–58.

Adams, Robert McC., and Hans J. Nissen. 1972. *The Uruk countryside: the natural setting of urban societies*. Chicago: University of Chicago Press.

Andrews, E. Wyllys. 1965. Archaeology and prehistory in the northern Maya Lowlands: an introduction. In *Handbook of Middle American Indians*, vol. 2, pt. 1, ed. Gordon R. Willey, pp. 288–330. Austin: University of Texas Press.

Balkansky, Andrew. 1997. Archaeological settlement patterns of the Sola Valley, Oaxaca, Mexico. *Mexicon* 19(1):12–19.

1998. Urbanism and early state formation in the Huamelulpan Valley of southern Mexico. *Latin American Antiquity* 9:37–76.

Beals, Ralph L. 1945. *Ethnology of the Western Mixe*. University of California Publications in American Archaeology and Ethnology 42.

1975. *The peasant marketing system of Oaxaca, Mexico*. Berkeley: University of California Press.

Berdan, Frances F. 1975. Trade, tribute and market in the Aztec empire. Ph.D. diss., University of Texas, Austin.

1980. Aztec merchants and markets: local-level economic activity in a non-industrial empire. *Mexicon* 2(3):37–41.

1982. *The Aztecs of Mexico: an imperial society*. New York: Holt, Rinehart and Winston.

1985. Markets in the economy of Aztec Mexico. In *Markets and marketing*, ed. Stuart Plattner, pp. 339–67. Society for Economic Anthropology Monographs in Economic Anthropology 4.

1988. Principles of regional and long-distance trade in the Aztec empire. In

136   Bibliography

Smoke and mist: Mesoamerican studies in memory of Thelma D. Sullivan, ed. J. Kathryn Josserand and Karen Dakin, pp. 639–56. British Archaeological Reports International Series 402.

Berdan, Frances F., and Patricia Rieff Anawalt. 1997. *The essential Codex Mendoza*. Berkeley: University of California Press.

Berdan, Frances F., Richard E. Blanton, Elizabeth Hill Boone, Mary G. Hodge, Michael E. Smith, and Emily Umberger. 1996. *Aztec imperial strategies*. Washington, D.C.: Dumbarton Oaks.

Bernal, Ignacio. 1965. Archaeological synthesis of Oaxaca. In *Handbook of Middle American Indians*, vol. 3, pt. 2, ed. Gordon Willey, pp. 788–813. Austin: University of Texas Press.

——— 1980. *A history of Mexican archaeology: the vanished civilizations of Middle America*. London: Thames and Hudson.

Berreman, Gerald D. 1978. Scale and social relations: thoughts and three examples. In *Scale and social organization*, ed. Frederik Barth, pp. 41–77. Oslo: Universitetsforlaget.

Blake, Michael. 1991. An emerging Early Formative chiefdom at Paso de la Amada, Chiapas, Mexico. In *The formation of complex society in southeastern Mesoamerica*, ed. William R. Fowler, pp. 27–46. Boca Raton: CRC Press.

Blanton, Richard E. 1978. *Monte Albán: settlement patterns at the ancient Zapotec capital*. New York: Academic Press.

——— 1983. Factors underlying the origin and evolution of market systems. In *Economic anthropology: topics and theories*, ed. Sutti Ortiz, pp. 51–66. Society for Economic Anthropology Monographs in Economic Anthropology 1.

——— 1989. Continuity and change in public architecture: Periods I through V of the Valley of Oaxaca, Mexico. In *Monte Albán's hinterland, pt. 2: pre-Hispanic settlement patterns in Tlacolula, Etla, and Ocotlán, the Valley of Oaxaca*, by Stephen A. Kowalewski, Gary M. Feinman, Laura Finsten, Richard E. Blanton, and Linda M. Nicholas, pp. 409–47. Museum of Anthropology, University of Michigan, Memoirs 23.

——— 1994. *Houses and households: a comparative study*. New York: Plenum Press.

——— 1996. The Basin of Mexico market system and the growth of empire. In *Aztec imperial strategies*, by Frances F. Berdan, Richard E. Blanton, Elizabeth Hill Boone, Mary G. Hodge, Michael E. Smith, and Emily Umberger, pp. 47–84. Washington, D.C.: Dumbarton Oaks.

Blanton, Richard E., and Gary M. Feinman. 1984. The Mesoamerican world-system. *American Anthropologist* 86:673–92.

Blanton, Richard E., Gary M. Feinman, Stephen A. Kowalewski, and Peter N. Peregrine. 1996. A dual-processual theory for the evolution of Mesoamerican civilization. *Current Anthropology* 37:1–14.

Blanton, Richard E., Laura Finsten, Stephen A. Kowalewski, and Gary M. Feinman. 1996. Migration and population change in the pre-Hispanic Valley of Oaxaca, Mexico. In *Arqueología mesoamericana: homenaje a William T. Sanders*, vol. 2, ed. Alba Guadalupe Mastache, Jeffrey R. Parsons, Robert S. Santley, and Mari Carmen Serra Puche, pp. 11–36. México D. F: Instituto Nacional de Antropología e Historia.

Blanton, Richard E., Stephen A. Kowalewski, Gary M. Feinman, and Jill Appel. 1982. *Monte Albán's hinterland, pt. 1: pre-Hispanic settlement patterns of the central and southern parts of the Valley of Oaxaca, Mexico.* Museum of Anthropology, University of Michigan, Memoirs 15.

Blanton, Richard E., Stephen A. Kowalewski, Gary M. Feinman, and Laura Finsten. 1993. *Ancient Mesoamerica: a comparison of change in three regions.* 2d ed. Cambridge: Cambridge University Press.

Blanton, Richard E., Peter N. Peregrine, Deborah Winslow, and Thomas D. Hall, eds. 1997. *Economic analysis beyond the local system.* Society for Economic Anthropology Monographs in Economic Anthropology 13.

Blitz, Jennifer. 1995. Dietary variability and social inequality at Monte Albán, Oaxaca, Mexico. Ph.D. diss., University of Wisconsin–Madison.

Blunden, Caroline, and Mark Elvin. 1983. *Cultural atlas of China.* New York: Facts on File.

Boserup, Ester. 1965. *The conditions of agricultural growth: the economics of agrarian change under population pressure.* Chicago: Aldine.

Bove, Frederick J. 1989. *Formative settlement patterns on the Pacific Coast of Guatemala: a spatial analysis of complex societal evolution.* British Archaeological Reports International Series 493.

Bowling, Kenneth R. 1991. *The creation of Washington, D.C.: the idea and location of the American capital.* Fairfax: George Mason University Press.

Braudel, Fernand. 1972. *The Mediterranean and the Mediterranean world in the age of Philip II.* 2 vols. New York: Harper and Row.

Brockington, Donald L. 1957. A brief report on an archaeological survey of the Oaxacan coast. *Mesoamerican Notes* 5:98–104.

———. 1973. *Archaeological investigations at Miahuatlán, Oaxaca.* Vanderbilt University Publications in Anthropology 7.

Brumfiel, Elizabeth M. 1987. Elite and utilitarian crafts in the Aztec state. In *Specialization, exchange, and complex societies,* ed. Elizabeth M. Brumfiel and Timothy K. Earle, pp. 102–18. Cambridge: Cambridge University Press.

Brumfiel, Elizabeth M., and Timothy K. Earle, eds. 1987. *Specialization, exchange, and complex societies.* Cambridge: Cambridge University Press.

Brunskill, R. W. 1987. *Illustrated handbook of vernacular architecture.* 3d ed. London: Faber and Faber.

Byland, Bruce E. 1980. Political and economic evolution in the Tamazulapan Valley, Mixteca Alta, Oaxaca, Mexico: a regional approach. Ph.D. diss., Pennsylvania State University.

Byland, Bruce E., and John M. Pohl. 1994. *In the realm of 8 Deer: the archaeology of the Mixtec codices.* Norman: University of Oklahoma Press.

Calnek, Edward E. 1976. The internal structure of Tenochtitlan. In *The Valley of Mexico: studies in pre-Hispanic ecology and society,* ed. Eric R. Wolf, pp. 287–302. Albuquerque: University of New Mexico Press.

———. 1978. The internal structure of cities in America: pre-Columbian cities, the case of Tenochtitlan. In *Urbanization in the Americas from its beginning to the present,* ed. Richard P. Schaedel, Jorge E. Hardoy, and Nora Scott Kinzer, pp. 315–26. The Hague: Mouton.

Cannon, Aubrey. 1989. The historical dimension in mortuary expressions of status and sentiment. *Current Anthropology* 30:437–58.

Carmona Macías, Martha, ed. 1989. *El Preclásico y Formativo: avances y perspectivas.* México, D.F: Instituto Nacional de Antropología e Historia.

Caso, Alfonso. 1928. *Las estelas Zapotecas*. México, D.F.: Secretaría de Educación Pública, Talleres Gráficos de la Nación.

1965a. Zapotec writing and calendar. In *Handbook of Middle American Indians*, vol. 3, pt. 2, ed. Gordon R. Willey, pp. 931–47. Austin: University of Texas Press.

1965b. Sculpture and mural painting of Oaxaca. In *Handbook of Middle American Indians*, vol. 3, pt. 2, ed. Gordon R. Willey, pp. 849–70. Austin: University of Texas Press.

1969. *El tesoro de Monte Albán*. Instituto Nacional de Antropología e Historia Memorias 3.

Caso, Alfonso, and Ignacio Bernal. 1952. *Urnas de Oaxaca*. Instituto Nacional de Antropología e Historia Memorias 11.

1965. Ceramics of Oaxaca. In *Handbook of Middle American Indians*, vol. 3, pt. 2, ed. Gordon R. Willey, pp. 871–95. Austin: University of Texas Press.

Caso, Alfonso, Ignacio Bernal, and Jorge R. Acosta. 1967. *La cerámica de Monte Albán*. Instituto Nacional de Antropología e Historia Memorias 13.

Chadwick, Robert. 1966. The tombs of Monte Albán I style at Yagul. In *Ancient Oaxaca: discoveries in Mexican archeology and history*, ed. John Paddock, pp. 245–55. Stanford: Stanford University Press.

Chandler, Tertius, and Gerald Fox. 1974. *3,000 years of urban growth*. New York: Academic Press.

Chang, Kwang-chih. 1986. *The archaeology of ancient China*. 4th ed. New Haven: Yale University Press.

Chase-Dunn, Christopher, and Thomas D. Hall. 1991a. Conceptualizing core/periphery hierarchies. In *Core/periphery relations in precapitalist worlds*, ed. Christopher Chase-Dunn and Thomas D. Hall, pp. 5–44. Boulder: Westview Press.

1997. *Rise and demise: comparing world-systems*. Boulder: Westview Press.

Chase-Dunn, Christopher, and Thomas D. Hall, eds. 1991b. *Core/periphery relations in precapitalist worlds*. Boulder: Westview Press.

Chisholm, Michael. 1968. *Rural settlement and land use: an essay in location*. 2d ed. London: Hutchinson University Library.

Claessen, Henri J., and Peter Skalník, eds. 1978. *The early state*. The Hague: Mouton.

Coe, Michael D. 1965a. Archaeological synthesis of southern Veracruz and Tabasco. In *Handbook of Middle American Indians*, vol. 3, pt. 2, ed. Gordon R. Willey, pp. 679–715. Austin: University of Texas Press.

1965b. The Olmec style and its distribution. In *Handbook of Middle American Indians*, vol. 3, pt. 2, ed. Gordon R. Willey, pp. 739–75. Austin: University of Texas Press.

1977. *Mexico*. 2d ed. New York: Praeger.

1981. Religion and the rise of Mesoamerican states. In *The transition to statehood in the New World*, ed. Grant D. Jones and Robert R. Kautz, pp. 157–71. Cambridge: Cambridge University Press.

1989. The Olmec heartland: evolution of ideology. In *Regional perspectives on the Olmec*, ed. Robert J. Sharer and David C. Grove, pp. 68–82. Cambridge: Cambridge University Press.

1994. *Mexico: from the Olmecs to the Aztecs*. London: Thames and Hudson.

Cook, Scott, and Martin Diskin, eds. 1976. *Markets in Oaxaca*. Austin: University of Texas Press.

Cowgill, George L. 1992. Toward a political history of Teotihuacan. In *Ideology and pre-Columbian civilizations*, ed. Arthur A. Demarest and Geoffrey W. Conrad, pp. 87–114. Santa Fe: School of American Research Press.

Curtin, Philip. 1984. *Cross-cultural trade in world history*. Cambridge: Cambridge University Press.

Dalton, George, ed. 1968. *Primitive, archaic, and modern economies: essays of Karl Polanyi*. Boston: Beacon Press.

Demand, Nancy H. 1990. *Urban relocation in Archaic and Classical Greece: flight and consolidation*. Norman: University of Oklahoma Press.

Demarest, Arthur A. 1989. The Olmec and the rise of civilization in eastern Mesoamerica. In *Regional perspectives on the Olmec*, ed. Robert J. Sharer and David C. Grove, pp. 303–44. Cambridge: Cambridge University Press.

Drennan, Robert D. 1976. *Fábrica San José and Middle Formative society in the Valley of Oaxaca*. Museum of Anthropology, University of Michigan, Memoirs 8.

1978. *Excavations at Quachilco: a report on the 1977 season of the Palo Blanco Project in the Tehuacan Valley*. Museum of Anthropology, University of Michigan, Technical Reports 7.

1979. *Prehistoric social, political, and economic development in the area of the Tehuacan Valley: some results of the Palo Blanco Project*. Museum of Anthropology, University of Michigan, Technical Reports 11.

1989. The mountains north of the valley. In *Monte Albán's hinterland, pt. 2: pre-Hispanic settlement patterns in Tlacolula, Etla, and Ocotlán, the Valley of Oaxaca*, by Stephen A. Kowalewski, Gary M. Feinman, Laura Finsten, Richard E. Blanton, and Linda M. Nicholas, pp. 367–84. Museum of Anthropology, University of Michigan, Memoirs 23.

Drennan, Robert D., and Kent V. Flannery. 1983. The growth of site hierarchies in the Valley of Oaxaca: part II. In *The cloud people: divergent evolution of the Zapotec and Mixtec civilizations*, ed. Kent V. Flannery and Joyce Marcus, pp. 65–71. New York: Academic Press.

Driver, Harold E. 1969. *Indians of North America*. 2d ed. Chicago: University of Chicago Press.

Drucker, Philip. 1943a. *Ceramic sequences at Tres Zapotes, Veracruz, Mexico*. Bureau of American Ethnology Bulletin 140.

1943b. *Ceramic stratigraphy at Cerro de las Mesas, Veracruz, Mexico*. Bureau of American Ethnology Bulletin 141.

1953. *La Venta, Tabasco: a study of Olmec ceramics and art*. Bureau of American Ethnology Bulletin 153.

Drucker, Philip, Robert F. Heizer, and Robert J. Squier. 1959. *Excavations at La Venta, Tabasco, 1955*. Bureau of American Ethnology Bulletin 170.

Earle, Timothy. 1978. *Economic and social organization of a complex chiefdom: the Halelea District, Kaua'i, Hawaii*. Museum of Anthropology, University of Michigan, Anthropological Papers 63.

1987. Specialization and the production of wealth: Hawaiian chiefdoms and the Inka empire. In *Specialization, exchange, and complex societies*, ed.

Elizabeth M. Brumfiel and Timothy K. Earle, pp. 64–75. Cambridge: Cambridge University Press.

Eggan, Fred. 1950. *Social organization of the Western Pueblos*. Chicago: University of Chicago Press.

Elam, J. Michael. 1989. Defensible and fortified sites. In *Monte Albán's hinterland, pt. 2: pre-Hispanic settlement patterns in Tlacolula, Etla, and Ocotlán, the Valley of Oaxaca*, by Stephen A. Kowalewski, Gary M. Feinman, Laura Finsten, Richard E. Blanton, and Linda M. Nicholas, pp. 385–407. Museum of Anthropology, University of Michigan, Memoirs 23.

Epstein, David G. 1973. *Brasília: plan and reality*. Berkeley: University of California Press.

Feder, Kenneth L. 1996. *Frauds, myths, and mysteries: science and pseudoscience in archaeology*. 2d ed. Mountain View, Calif.: Mayfield.

Feinman, Gary M. 1980. The relationship between administrative organization and ceramic production in the Valley of Oaxaca, Mexico. Ph.D. diss., City University of New York.

——— 1982. Patterns of ceramic production and distribution: periods Early I through V. In *Monte Albán's hinterland, pt. 1: pre-Hispanic settlement patterns of the central and southern parts of the Valley of Oaxaca, Mexico*, by Richard E. Blanton, Stephen A. Kowalewski, Gary M. Feinman, and Jill Appel, pp. 181–206. Museum of Anthropology, University of Michigan, Memoirs 15.

——— 1986. The emergence of specialized ceramic production in Formative Oaxaca. In *Economic aspects of pre-Hispanic highland Mexico*, ed. B. L. Isaac, pp. 347–73. Research in Economic Anthropology, suppl. 2.

——— 1991. Demography, surplus, and inequality: early political formations in highland Mesoamerica. In *Chiefdoms and their evolutionary significance*, ed. Timothy K. Earle, pp. 229–62. Cambridge: Cambridge University Press.

Feinman, Gary M., Richard E. Blanton, and Stephen A. Kowalewski. 1984. Market system development in the pre-Hispanic Valley of Oaxaca, Mexico. In *Trade and exchange in early Mesoamerica*, ed. Kenneth Hirth, pp. 157–78. Albuquerque: University of New Mexico Press.

Feinman, Gary M., Stephen A. Kowalewski, Laura Finsten, Richard E. Blanton, and Linda Nicholas. 1985. Long-term demographic change: a perspective from the Valley of Oaxaca, Mexico. *Journal of Field Archaeology* 12: 333–62.

Feinman, Gary M., and Jill Neitzel. 1984. Too many types: an overview of sedentary prestate societies in the Americas. *Advances in Archaeological Method and Theory* 7: 39–102.

Feinman, Gary M., and Linda M. Nicholas. 1987. Labor, surplus, and production: a regional analysis of Formative Oaxacan socio-economic change. In *Coasts, plains, and deserts: essays in honor of Reynold J. Ruppé*, ed. Sylvia W. Gaines, pp. 27–50. Arizona State University, Anthropological Research Papers 38.

——— 1990a. At the margins of the Monte Albán state: settlement patterns in the Ejutla Valley, Oaxaca, Mexico. *Latin American Antiquity* 1: 216–46.

——— 1990b. Settlement and land use in ancient Oaxaca. In *Debating Oaxaca archaeology*, ed. Joyce Marcus, pp. 71–113. Museum of Anthropology, University of Michigan, Anthropological Papers 84.

1996. Defining the eastern limits of the Monte Albán state: systematic settle-ment pattern survey in the Guirún area, Oaxaca, Mexico. *Mexicon* 18 (5): 91–97.

Finsten, Laura. 1996. Frontier and periphery in southern Mexico: the Mixtec sierra in highland Oaxaca. In *Pre-Columbian world systems*, ed. Peter N. Peregrine and Gary M. Feinman, pp. 77–95. Madison: Prehistory Press.

Fischer, K. F. 1984. *Canberra, myths and models: forces at work in the formation of the Australian capital*. Hamburg: Institute of Asian Affairs.

Flannery, Kent V. 1972. The cultural evolution of civilizations. *Annual Review of Ecology and Systematics* 3:399–426.

1976. Contextual analysis of ritual paraphernalia from Formative Oaxaca. In *The early Mesoamerican village*, ed. Kent V. Flannery, pp. 333–45. New York: Academic Press.

1982. Review of *In the land of the Olmec*, by Michael Coe and Richard Diehl. *American Anthropologist* 84:442–47.

Flannery, Kent V., ed. 1976. *The early Mesoamerican village*. New York: Academic Press.

Flannery, Kent V., Anne V. T. Kirkby, Michael J. Kirkby, and Aubrey W. Williams Jr. 1967. Farming systems and political growth in ancient Oaxaca. *Science* 158:445–54.

Flannery, Kent V., and Joyce Marcus. 1983. The growth of site hierarchies in the Valley of Oaxaca: part I. In *The cloud people: divergent evolution of the Zapotec and Mixtec civilizations*, ed. Kent V. Flannery and Joyce Marcus, pp. 53–64. New York: Academic Press.

1994. *Early Formative pottery of the Valley of Oaxaca*. Museum of Anthropology, University of Michigan, Memoirs 27.

Flannery, Kent V., and Joyce Marcus, eds. 1983. *The cloud people: divergent evolution of the Zapotec and Mixtec civilizations*. New York: Academic Press.

Forsyth, Donald W. 1989. *The ceramics of El Mirador, Petén, Guatemala: El Mirador series, pt. 4*. New World Archaeological Foundation, Paper 63.

Frank, Andre Gunder. 1969. *Capitalism and underdevelopment in Latin America: historical studies of Chile and Brazil*. 2d ed. New York: Monthly Review Press.

Frank, Andre Gunder, and Barry K. Gills, eds. 1993. *The world system: five hundred years or five thousand?* London: Routledge.

Freidel, David A., and Linda Schele. 1988. Kingship in the Late Preclassic Maya Lowlands: the instruments and places of ritual power. *American Anthropologist* 90:547–67.

Fried, Morton H. 1967. *The evolution of political society: an essay in political anthro-pology*. New York: Random House.

García Cook, Angel 1981. The historical importance of Tlaxcala in the cultural development of the central highlands. In *Supplement to the Handbook of Middle American Indians*, vol. 1, ed. Victoria R. Bricker and Jeremy A. Sabloff, pp. 244–76. Austin: University of Texas Press.

García Payón, José. 1965. Archaeology of central Veracruz. In *Handbook of Middle American Indians*, vol. 11, ed. Gordon F. Ekholm and Ignacio Bernal, pp. 505–42. Austin: University of Texas Press.

Gaxiola González, Margarita. 1984. *Huamelulpan: un centro urbano de la Mixteca Alta*. México, D.F.: Instituto Nacional de Antropología e Historia.

Gerhard, Peter. 1972. *A guide to the historical geography of New Spain.* Cambridge: Cambridge University Press.

Gillespie, Susan D. 1993. Power, pathways, and appropriations in Mesoamerican art. In *Imagery and creativity: ethnoaesthetics and art worlds in the Americas,* ed. Dorothea S. Whitten and Norman E. Whitten Jr., pp. 67–107. Tucson: University of Arizona Press.

Gills, Barry K., and Andre Gunder Frank. 1991. 5,000 years of world system history: the cumulation of accumulation. In *Core/periphery relations in precapitalist worlds,* ed. Christopher Chase-Dunn and Thomas D. Hall, pp. 67–112. Boulder: Westview Press.

Grove, David C. 1987. Chalcatzingo in a broader perspective. In *Ancient Chalzatzingo,* ed. David C. Grove, pp. 434–42. Austin: University of Texas Press.

——— 1997. Olmec archaeology: a half century of research and its accomplishments. *Journal of World Prehistory* 11:51–101.

Guthe, H. 1959. Jerusalem. In *The new Schaff-Herzog encyclopedia of religious knowledge,* ed. Samuel M. Jackson, pp. 130–35. Grand Rapids, Mich.: Baker Book House.

Haas, Jonathan. 1982. *The evolution of the prehistoric state.* New York: Columbia University Press.

Haggett, Peter. 1966. *Locational analysis in human geography.* New York: St. Martin's Press.

Hall, Thomas D. 1986. Incorporation in the world-system: toward a critique. *American Sociological Review* 51:390–402.

——— 1997. The millennium before the "long sixteenth century": how many world-systems were there? In *Economic analysis beyond the local system,* ed. Richard E. Blanton, Peter N. Peregrine, Deborah Winslow, and Thomas D. Hall, pp. 43–69. Society for Economic Anthropology Monographs in Economic Anthropology 13.

Hall, Thomas D., and Christopher Chase-Dunn. 1993. The world-systems perspective and archaeology: forward into the past. *Journal of Archaeological Research* 1:121–43.

Helms, Mary W. 1979. *Ancient Panama: chiefs in search of power.* Austin: University of Texas Press.

——— 1988. *Ulysses' sail.* Cambridge: Cambridge University Press.

Hignett, C. 1958. *A history of the Athenian constitution to the end of the fifth century, B. C.* Oxford: Oxford University Press.

Hirth, Kenneth G. 1987. Formative period settlement patterns in the Río Amatzinac Valley. In *Ancient Chalzatzingo,* ed. David C. Grove, pp. 343–67. Austin: University of Texas Press.

Hodge, Mary G. 1996. Political organization of the central provinces. In *Aztec imperial strategies,* by Frances F. Berdan, Richard E. Blanton, Elizabeth Hill Boone, Mary G. Hodge, Michael E. Smith, and Emily Umberger, pp. 17–46. Washington, D.C.: Dumbarton Oaks.

Hodges, Denise C. 1989. *Agricultural intensification and prehistoric health in the Valley of Oaxaca, Mexico.* Museum of Anthropology, University of Michigan, Memoirs 22.

Hoebel, E. Adamson. 1978. *The Cheyennes: Indians of the Great Plains.* 2d ed. New York: Holt, Rinehart and Winston.

Holmes, William H. 1895–97. *Archaeological studies among the ancient cities of Mexico*. Field Museum Anthropological Series 1(1).

Hosler, Dorothy. 1988. The metallurgy of ancient West Mexico. In *The beginning of the use of metals and alloys*, ed. Robert Maddin, pp. 328–43. Cambridge, Mass.: MIT Press.

Humphrey, Caroline, and Stephen Hugh-Jones, eds. 1992. *Barter, exchange, and value: an anthropological approach*. Cambridge: Cambridge University Press.

Hunt, Eva, and Robert Hunt. 1974. Irrigation, conflict, and politics: a Mexican case. In *Irrigation's impact on society*, ed. Theodore Downing and McGuire Gibson, pp. 129–57. Tucson: University of Arizona Press.

Hunt, Eva, and June Nash. 1967. Local and territorial units. In *Handbook of Middle American Indians*, vol. 6, ed. Manning Nash, pp. 253–82. Austin: University of Texas Press.

Johnson, Allen W., and Timothy Earle. 1987. *The evolution of human societies: from foraging group to agrarian state*. Stanford: Stanford University Press.

Johnson, Gregory. 1973. *Local exchange and early state development in southwestern Iran*. Museum of Anthropology, University of Michigan, Anthropological Papers 51.

1987. The changing organization of Uruk administration on the Susiana Plain. In *The archaeology of western Iran: settlement and society from prehistory to the Islamic conquest*, ed. Frank Hole, pp. 107–40. Washington, D.C.: Smithsonian Institution Press.

Joyce, Arthur. 1993. Interregional interaction and social development on the Oaxaca coast. *Ancient Mesoamerica* 4:67–84.

Joyce, Arthur A., and Marcus Winter. 1996. Ideology, power, and urban society in pre-Hispanic Oaxaca. *Current Anthropology* 37:33–47.

Kardulias, P. Nick. 1990. Fur production as a specialized activity in a world system: Indians in the North American fur trade. *American Indian Culture and Research Journal* 14:25–60.

Kemp, Barry J. 1989. *Ancient Egypt: anatomy of a civilization*. London: Routledge.

Kirkby, Anne V. T. 1973. *The use of land and water resources in the past and present Valley of Oaxaca*. Museum of Anthropology, University of Michigan, Memoirs 5.

Knight, David B. 1977a. *Choosing Canada's capital: jealousy and friction in the nineteenth century*. Ottawa: Carleton University Press.

1977b. *A capital for Canada: conflict and compromise in the nineteenth century*. University of Chicago Department of Geography, Geography Research Paper 182.

Kowalewski, Stephen A. 1997. A spatial method for integrating data of different types. *Journal of Anthropological Method and Theory* 4(3/4):287–306.

Kowalewski, Stephen A., Gary M. Feinman, Laura Finsten, Richard E. Blanton, and Linda M. Nicholas. 1989. *Monte Albán's hinterland, pt. 2: pre-Hispanic settlement patterns in Tlacolula, Etla, and Ocotlán, the Valley of Oaxaca*. Museum of Anthropology, University of Michigan, Memoirs 23.

Kowalewski, Stephen A., and Laura M. Finsten. 1983. The economic systems of ancient Oaxaca: a regional perspective. *Current Anthropology* 24:413–41.

Kowalewski, Stephen A., Charles Spencer, and Elsa Redmond. 1978. Description of ceramic categories. In *Monte Albán: settlement patterns at the ancient Zapotec capital*, by Richard E. Blanton, pp. 167–94. New York: Academic Press.

Kroeber, Alfred L. 1952. *The nature of culture.* Chicago: University of Chicago Press.

Kuper, Adam, ed. 1977. *The social anthropology of Radcliffe-Brown.* London: Routledge and Kegan Paul.

Leacock, Eleanor Burke, ed. 1972. *The origin of the family, private property, and the state, by Frederick Engels.* New York: International Publishers.

Lee, Thomas A., Jr. 1969. *The artifacts of Chiapa de Corzo, Chiapas, Mexico.* New World Archaeological Foundation Paper 26.

Lees, Susan. 1973. *Sociopolitical aspects of canal irrigation in the Valley of Oaxaca, Mexico.* Museum of Anthropology, University of Michigan, Memoirs 6.

Lewis, Oscar. 1942. *The effects of white contact upon Blackfoot culture: with special reference to the role of the fur trade.* Monographs of the American Ethnological Society 6.

Love, Michael W. 1991. Style and social complexity in Formative Mesoamerica. In *The formation of complex society in southeastern Mesoamerica*, ed. William R. Fowler, pp. 47–76. Boca Raton: CRC Press.

Lowe, Gareth W., Thomas A. Lee Jr., and Eduardo Martínez Espinosa. 1982. *Izapa: an introduction to the ruins and monuments.* New World Archaeological Foundation Paper 31.

Lowell, Julia C. 1996. Moieties in prehistory: a case study from the Pueblo Southwest. *Journal of Field Archaeology* 23:77–90.

McDonald, Andrew J. 1983. *Tzutzuculi: a Middle-Preclassic site on the Pacific Coast of Chiapas, Mexico.* New World Archaeological Foundation Paper 47.

McNeill, William H. 1991. *The rise of the West: a history of the human community.* Chicago: University of Chicago Press.

MacNeish, Richard S., Melvin L. Fowler, Angel García Cook, Frederick A. Peterson, Antoinette Nelken-Turner, and James A. Neely. 1972. *The pre-history of the Tehuacan Valley.* vol. 5: *Excavations and reconnaissance.* Austin: University of Texas Press.

Malinowski, Bronislaw. 1922. *Argonauts of the Western Pacific.* London: Routledge.

Manzanilla, Linda, and Leonardo López Luján, eds. 1994. *Historia antigua de México,* Vol. 1. *El México antiguo, sus áreas culturales, los orígenes y el horizonte Preclásico.* México, D.F.: Instituto Nacional de Antropología e Historia.

Marcus, Joyce. 1976. The iconography of militarism at Monte Albán and neighboring sites in the Valley of Oaxaca. In *Origins of religious art and iconography in Preclassic Mesoamerica*, ed. Henry B. Nicholson, pp. 123–39. Los Angeles: UCLA Latin American Center.

1980. Zapotec writing. *Scientific American* 242:50–64.

1983a. Stone monuments and tomb murals of Monte Albán IIIa. In *The cloud people: divergent evolution of the Zapotec and Mixtec civilizations*, ed. Kent V. Flannery and Joyce Marcus, pp. 137–43. New York: Academic Press.

1983b. Teotihuacan visitors on Monte Albán monuments and murals. In *The cloud people: divergent evolution of the Zapotec and Mixtec civilizations*, ed. Kent V. Flannery and Joyce Marcus, pp. 175–80. New York: Academic Press.

1983c. Lintel 2 at Xoxocotlán. In *The cloud people: divergent evolution of the Zapotec and Mixtec civilizations*, ed. Kent V. Flannery and Joyce Marcus, pp. 150–52. New York: Academic Press.

1989. Zapotec chiefdoms and the nature of Formative religions. In *Regional perspectives on the Olmec*, ed. Robert J. Sharer and David C. Grove, pp. 148–97. Cambridge: Cambridge University Press.

1992. *Mesoamerican writing systems: propaganda, myth, and history in four ancient civilizations*. Princeton: Princeton University Press.

1993. Ancient Maya political organization. In *Lowland Maya civilization in the eighth century*, ed. Jeremy A. Sabloff and John S. Henderson, pp. 111–83. Washington, D.C.: Dumbarton Oaks.

Marcus, Joyce, and Gary M. Feinman, eds. 1998. *The archaic state*. Santa Fe: School of American Research Press.

Marcus, Joyce, and Kent V. Flannery. 1994. Ancient Zapotec ritual and religion: an application of the direct historical approach. In *The ancient mind*, ed. Colin Renfrew and Ezra Zubrow, pp. 55–74. Cambridge: Cambridge University Press.

1996. *Zapotec civilization: how urban society evolved in Mexico's Oaxaca Valley*. London: Thames and Hudson.

Markman, Charles W. 1981. *Pre-Hispanic settlement dynamics in central Oaxaca, Mexico: a view from the Miahuatlán Valley*. Vanderbilt University Publications in Anthropology 26.

Marquina, Ignacio. 1964. *Arquitectura prehispánica*. Instituto Nacional de Antropología e Historia Memorias 1.

Miller, Walter B. 1955. Two concepts of authority. *American Anthropologist* 57:271–89.

Millon, René. 1973. *Urbanization at Teotihuacan*, vol. 1. *The Teotihuacan map*, pt. 1, *Text*. Austin: University of Texas Press.

Monaghan, John. 1990. Sacrifice, death, and the origins of agriculture in the Codex Vienna. *American Antiquity* 55:559–69.

Murra, John V. 1980. *The economic organization of the Inka state*. Research in Economic Anthropology suppl. 1.

Nabokov, Peter. 1989. *Native American architecture*. Oxford: Oxford University Press.

Nicholas, Linda M. 1989. Land use in pre-Hispanic Oaxaca. In *Monte Albán's hinterland, pt. 2: pre-Hispanic settlement patterns in Tlacolula, Etla, and Ocotlán, the Valley of Oaxaca*, by Stephen A. Kowalewski, Gary M. Feinman, Laura Finsten, Richard E. Blanton, and Linda M. Nicholas, pp. 449–505. Museum of Anthropology, University of Michigan, Memoirs 23.

Nicholas, Linda M., Gary M. Feinman, Stephen A. Kowalewski, Richard E. Blanton, and Laura Finsten. 1986. Pre-Hispanic colonization of the Valley of Oaxaca, Mexico. *Human Ecology* 14:131–62.

Nicholson, Henry B. 1971. Religion in pre-Hispanic central Mexico. In *Handbook of Middle American Indians*, vol. 10, pt. 1, ed. Gordon Ekholm and Ignacio Bernal, pp. 395–446. Austin: University of Texas Press.

O'Brien, Michael J., Roger Mason, Dennis Lewarch, and James Neely. 1982. *A Late Formative irrigation settlement below Monte Albán: survey and excavation on the Xoxocotlán piedmont, Oaxaca, Mexico*. Austin: University of Texas Press.

Ortiz, Alfonso, ed. 1979. *Handbook of North American Indians*, vol. 9. Washington, D.C.: Smithsonian Institution Press.

Paddock, John, ed. 1966. *Ancient Oaxaca*. Stanford: Stanford University Press.

Parsons, Jeffrey R. 1971. *Prehistoric settlement patterns of the Texcoco region, Mexico.* Museum of Anthropology, University of Michigan, Memoirs 3.

Pasztory, Esther. 1997. *Teotihuacan: an experiment in living.* Norman: University of Oklahoma Press.

Payne, William O. 1994. The raw materials and pottery-making techniques of Early Formative Oaxaca: an introduction. In *Early Formative pottery of the Valley of Oaxaca,* by Kent V. Flannery and Joyce Marcus, pp. 7–20. Museum of Anthropology, University of Michigan, Memoirs 27.

Peregrine, Peter N., and Gary M. Feinman, eds. 1996. *Pre-Columbian world systems.* Madison: Prehistory Press.

Pires-Ferreira, Jane W. 1975. *Formative Mesoamerican exchange networks with special reference to the Valley of Oaxaca.* Museum of Anthropology, University of Michigan, Memoirs 7.

1976. Shell and iron-ore mirror exchange in Formative Mesoamerica, with comments on other commodities. In *The Early Mesoamerican village,* ed. Kent V. Flannery, pp. 311–28. New York: Academic Press.

Pollard, Helen P. 1993. *Tariacuri's legacy: the pre-Hispanic Tarascan state.* Norman: University of Oklahoma Press.

Pospisil, Leopold. 1963. *The Kapauku Papuans of West New Guinea.* New York: Holt, Rinehart, and Winston.

Price, T. Douglas, and Gary M. Feinman, eds. 1995. *Foundations of social inequality.* New York: Plenum Press.

Pye, Mary E., and Arthur A. Demarest. 1991. The evolution of complex societies in southeastern Mesoamerica: new evidence from El Mesak, Guatemala. In *The formation of complex society in southeastern Mesoamerica,* ed. William R. Fowler, pp. 77–100. Boca Raton: CRC Press.

Pyne, Nanette M. 1976. The fire-serpent and were-jaguar in Formative Oaxaca: a contingency table analysis. In *The Early Mesoamerican village,* ed. Kent V. Flannery, pp. 272–82. New York: Academic Press.

Redmond, Elsa M. 1983. *A fuego y sangre: early Zapotec imperialism in the Cuicatlán Cañada.* Museum of Anthropology, University of Michigan, Memoirs 16.

Sanders, William T. 1965. *The cultural ecology of the Teotihuacan Valley.* Ms, Department of Anthropology, Pennsylvania State University, University Park, Pa.

Sanders, William T., and Deborah L. Nichols. 1988. Ecological theory and cultural evolution in the Valley of Oaxaca. *Current Anthropology* 29:33–80.

Sanders, William T., Jeffrey R. Parsons, and Robert S. Santley. 1979. *The Basin of Mexico: ecological processes in the evolution of a civilization.* New York: Academic Press.

Sanders, William T., and Barbara J. Price. 1968. *Mesoamerica: the evolution of a civilization.* New York: Random House.

Sanderson, Stephen K. ed. 1995. *Civilizations and world systems: studying world-historical change.* Walnut Creek, Calif.: Alta Mira Press.

Santley, Robert S., and Philip J. Arnold III. 1996. Pre-Hispanic settlement patterns in the Tuxtla Mountains, southern Veracruz. *Journal of Field Archaeology* 23:225–49.

Schele, Linda, and Mary Ellen Miller. 1986. *Blood of kings: dynasty and ritual in Maya art.* New York: Georges Braziller.

Schneider, Jane. 1977. Was there a precapitalist world-system? *Peasant Studies* 6:20–9.

Schortman, Edward M., and Patricia A. Urban. 1991. Patterns of Late Preclassic interaction and the formation of complex society in the southwest Maya periphery. In *The formation of complex society in southeastern Mesoamerica*, ed. William R. Fowler, pp. 121–42. Boca Raton: CRC Press.

Schortman, Edward M., and Patricia A. Urban, eds. 1992. *Resources, power, and interregional interaction*. New York: Plenum Press.

Scott, John F. 1978. *The danzantes of Monte Albán*, 2 pts. Washington, D.C.: Dumbarton Oaks.

Service, Elman R. 1971. *Primitive social organization: an evolutionary perspective*. 2d ed. New York: Random House.

   1975. *Origins of the state and civilization: the process of cultural evolution*. New York: W. W. Norton.

Sharer, Robert J. 1994. *The ancient Maya*. 5th ed. Stanford: Stanford University Press.

Sharer, Robert J., and David C. Grove, eds. 1989. *Regional perspectives on the Olmec*. Cambridge: Cambridge University Press.

Smith, Mary Elizabeth. 1973. *Picture writing from ancient southern Mexico: Mixtec place signs and maps*. Norman: University of Oklahoma Press.

Smith, Michael E. 1996a. *The Aztecs*. Oxford: Blackwell.

   1996b. The strategic provinces. In *Aztec imperial strategies*, by Frances F. Berdan, Richard E. Blanton, Elizabeth Hill Boone, Mary G. Hodge, Michael E. Smith, and Emily Umberger, pp. 137–50. Washington, D.C.: Dumbarton Oaks.

Smith, Michael E., and Cynthia Heath-Smith. 1980. Waves of influence in Postclassic Mesoamerica? A critique of the Mixteca-Puebla concept. *Anthropology* 4:15–50.

   1994. Rural economy in Late Postclassic Morelos: an archaeological study. In *Economies and polities in the Aztec realm*, ed. Mary G. Hodge and Michael E. Smith, pp. 349–76. Albany: State University of New York.

Snodgrass, Anthony. 1980. *Archaic Greece: the age of experiment*. Berkeley: University of California Press.

Spence, Michael W., and Jeffrey R. Parsons. 1972. Pre-Hispanic obsidian exploitation in central Mexico: a preliminary synthesis. In *Miscellaneous studies in Mexican prehistory*, by Michael W. Spence, Jeffrey R. Parsons, and Mary Hrones Parsons, pp. 1–44. Museum of Anthropology, University of Michigan, Anthropological Papers 45.

Spencer, Charles S., 1982. *The Cuicatlán Cañada and Monte Albán: a study of primary state formation*. New York: Academic Press.

   1993. Human agency, biased transmission, and the cultural evolution of chiefly authority. *Journal of Anthropological Archaeology* 12:41–74.

Spencer, Charles S., and Elsa M. Redmond. 1997. *Archaeology of the Cañada de Cuicatlán, Oaxaca*. American Museum of Natural History.

Spores, Ronald. 1972. *An archaeological settlement survey of the Nochixtlán Valley, Oaxaca*. Vanderbilt University Publications in Anthropology 1.

Stark, Barbara L., ed. 1991. *Settlement archaeology of Cerro de las Mesas, Veracruz, Mexico*. Los Angeles: Institute of Archaeology, University of California.

Stirling, Matthew W. 1965. Monumental sculpture of southern Veracruz and Tabasco. In *Handbook of Middle American Indians*, vol. 3, pt. 2, ed. Gordon R. Willey, pp. 716–38. Austin: University of Texas Press.

Strouhal, Eugen. 1992. *Life of the ancient Egyptians*. Norman: University of Oklahoma Press.

Súarez, Jorge A. 1983. *The Mesoamerican Indian languages*. Cambridge: Cambridge University Press.

Titiev, Mischa. 1944. *Old Oraibi*. Peabody Museum of American Archaeology and Ethnology, Paper 22(1).

Trigger, Bruce G. 1990. Maintaining economic equality in opposition to complexity: an Iroquoian case study. In *The evolution of political systems: sociopolitics in small-scale sedentary societies*, ed. Steadman Upham, pp. 119–45. Cambridge: Cambridge University Press.

Urcid, Javier. 1994. Un sistema de nomenclatura para los monolitos grabados y los materiales con inscripciones de Monte Albán. In *Escritura Zapoteca prehispánica*, ed. Marcus Winter, pp. 53–80. Oaxaca: Instituto Nacional de Antropología e Historia, Centro Oaxaca.

Vaillant, George C. 1931. Excavations at Ticoman. *Anthropological Papers of the American Museum of Natural History* 32(2):198–451.

Wallerstein, Immanuel. 1974. *The modern world-system: capitalist agriculture and the origins of the European world-economy in the sixteenth century*. New York: Academic Press.

Walton, William. 1966. *The evidence of Washington*. New York: Harper and Row.

Weaver, Muriel, P. 1993. *The Aztecs, Maya, and their predecessors: archaeology of Mesoamerica*. 3d ed. New York: Academic Press.

Weiant, C. W. 1943. *An introduction to the ceramics of Tres Zapotes, Veracruz, Mexico*. Bureau of American Ethnology Bulletin 139.

Whalen, Michael E. 1981. *Excavations at Santo Domingo Tomaltepec: evolution of a Formative community in the Valley of Oaxaca, Mexico*. Museum of Anthropology, University of Michigan, Memoirs 12.

1988. House and households in Formative Oaxaca. In *Household and community in the Mesoamerican past*, ed. Richard R. Wilk and Wendy Ashmore, pp. 249–72. Albuquerque: University of New Mexico Press.

Whitecotton, Joseph W. 1977. *The Zapotecs: princes, priests, and peasants*. Norman: University of Oklahoma Press.

Winter, Marcus C. 1972. Tierras Largas: a Formative community in the Valley of Oaxaca, Mexico. Ph.D. diss., University of Arizona.

1974. Residential patterns at Monte Albán, Oaxaca, Mexico. *Science* 186:981–87.

1976. The archaeological household cluster in the Valley of Oaxaca. In *The early Mesoamerican village*, ed. Kent V. Flannery, pp. 25–34. New York: Academic Press.

1984. Exchange in Formative highland Oaxaca. In *Trade and exchange in early Mesoamerica*, ed. Kenneth Hirth, pp. 179–214. Albuquerque: University of New Mexico Press.

1989. *Oaxaca: the archaeological record*. México, D. F.: Minutiae Mexicana.

Wittfogel, Karl. 1957. *Oriental despotism*. New Haven: Yale University Press.

Wolf, Eric R. 1959. *Sons of the shaking earth.* Chicago: University of Chicago Press.

1982. *Europe and the people without history.* Berkeley: University of California Press.

Wonderley, Anthony. 1991. The Late Preclassic Sula Plain, Honduras: regional antecedents to social complexity and interregional convergence in ceramic style. In *The formation of complex society in southeastern Mesoamerica,* ed. William R. Fowler, pp. 143–70. Boca Raton: CRC Press.

Wright, Henry T. 1969. *The administration of production in an early Mesopotamian town.* Museum of Anthropology, University of Michigan, Anthropological Papers 38.

1986. The evolution of civilizations. In *American archaeology past and future,* ed. David J. Meltzer, Don D. Fowler, and Jeremy Sabloff, pp. 323–65. Washington, D.C.: Smithsonian Institution Press.

Wright, Henry T., and Gregory Johnson. 1975. Population, exchange, and early state formation in southwestern Iran. *American Anthropologist* 77:267–89.

Yoffee, Norman. 1993. Mesopotamian interaction spheres. In *Early stages in the evolution of Mesopotamian civilization,* ed. Norman Yoffee and Jeffrey J. Clark, pp. 257–70. Tucson: University of Arizona Press.

Zárate, Roberto. 1987. *Excavaciones de un sitio preclásico en San Mateo Etlatongo, Nochixtlán, Oaxaca, México.* British Archaeological Reports International Series 322.

Zeitlin, Judith F. 1978. Community distribution and local economy on the southern Isthmus of Tehuantepec: archaeological and ethnohistorical investigation. Ph.D. diss., Yale University.

Zeitlin, Robert N. 1978. Long-distance exchange and the growth of a regional center on the southern Isthmus of Tehuantepec, Mexico. In *Prehistoric coastal adaptations: the economy and ecology of maritime Middle America,* ed. Barbara L. Stark and Barbara Voorhies, pp. 183–210. New York: Academic Press.

1993. Pacific coastal Laguna Zope: a regional center in the Terminal Formative hinterlands of Monte Albán. *Ancient Mesoamerica* 4:85–101.

Index

Acosta, Jorge R., 134
agriculture, 2, 13, 20
  during Early I, 89–92, 94–5, 108
  during the Early and Middle Formative,
    88–9
  during Late I, 92–5, 108
  and state formation, 115–18
  in the Valley of Oaxaca, 25, 26, 28,
    31–4, 49–52, 66
Altar de Sacrificios, 125
ancestor veneration, 2, 46
Appel, Jill, 134
Athens, 63, 65
Aztec, 1, 9, 11, 12, 15–16, 23, 58, 133

Basin of Mexico, 15, 20–1, 46, 71, 121,
  123, 125
Berdan, Frances F., 133
Bernal, Ignacio, 22, 24, 134
big-man societies, 39
Blanton, Richard E., 24, 60, 133,
  134
boundary sites, 122, 126
  in Aztec empire, 16, 127
boundedness, 68, 121, 126–7
Braudel, Fernand, 5
Brasília, 66
Brockington, Donald L., 25, 29
buffer zones, 42–4
burials 29, 35, 38, 39, 46, 88, 104–5, 125,
  127, 131

Canberra, Australia, 65
carved-stone monuments, 44–5, 62, 124,
  129, *see also* Danzantes
Caso, Alfonso, 22–3, 129, 134
central highlands of Mexico, 9
ceramics, 13–14, 42, 48, 49, 53, 61, 95–9,
  101–7, 109, 131, 132
Cerro de las Mesas, 124
Chalcatzingo, 18, 20, 46, 123
Chase-Dunn, Christopher, 134
Chiapa de Corzo, 124–5

chiefdom, 3, 36–9, 40, 41, 42, 46, 112,
  122, 130–1
China, 1, 4, 108, 113, 115, 120
civilizations, 4–7, 16–17, *see also* China,
  Egypt, Mesoamerica
Cocijo, 103, 105–7, 120, 128, 131
Coe, Michael, 62, 133
comal, 95–6, 123, 131
communications functionalism, 119–20
complexity, 68
conflict, 113–14, 117
core–periphery interactions, 6, 15, *see also*
  exchange of goods, world-systems
  theory
corporate governance, 41, 42, 129
craft specialization, 2, 15, 20, 97–9, 105,
  109, 119
Cuello, 125
Cuicatlán Cañada, 25, 29, 122
Cuicuilco, 123
cultural ecology, 114–18

Danzantes, 62, 64, 82, 114, 125
descent groups, 37–9, 41
diet, 29
diffusion, 112–13
disembedded capital, 65–6
Drennan, Robert, 134

Earle, Timothy, 134
Early Formative period
  in Mesoamerica, 17–20
  in the Valley of Oaxaca, 34–42
Early Horizon, 17–20, 34, 46, 121, 133
Eggan, Fred, 40
Egypt, 1, 4, 112, 113, 128, 129
Ejutla Valley, 25, 31, 91, 94, 110, 121,
  122, 126
El Mirador, 125
El Trapiche, 124
Engels, Frederick, 113, 134
Etla Valley, *see* Valley of Oaxaca
exchange of goods

in the Early and Middle Formative, 18,
20, 35, 39, 42, 46, 99
in markets, 2, 11, 15, 20, 60, 100, 118,
119
in the Middle Horizon, 42
in a redistributive economy, 100, 118–19
in world-systems, 6, 15, 21, 126–7
see also prestige goods

Fábrica San José, 23, 104, 134
Feinman, Gary M., 133, 134
Finsten, Laura M., 133, 134
Flannery, Kent V., 23, 24, 133, 134
food preparation, 38, 94–6, 105
Fried, Morton, 134
functionalism, 118–20

Gills, Barry K., 6
Greece, 63–5
Grove, David C., 133
Guirún, 25, 91, 94, 110, 121, 122, 126
Gunder Frank, A. 5, 6

Haas, Jonathan, 134
Hague confederacy, 66
Hall, Thomas D., 134
health, 29, 53, 95, 108
hierarchy, 3, 68–70, 87–8
civic-ceremonial, 69, 77–87, 127
of settlements, 70–7
in states, 3, 13
in world-systems, 6
Hopi, 39
households, 2, 15, 37, 38–9, 53, 58, 60–1,
94–100, 107–10, 117, 119, 122, 127
houses, 2, 35–6, 37, 45–6, 56–60, 71, 79,
109–10, 114, 131
Huamelulpan, 122, 124, 125
Huitzo, 23, 42, 122
Huixtepec, San Pablo, 82, 83
Huron, 35, 39

Inca, 1, 118, 119
Indus Valley, 113
inequality, 2, 13, 18, 20, 46, 133
in power, 36, 41, 42, 46
in prestige, 36–9, 41, 42
as ranking, 37–9, 46, 88, 130
in San José phase, 35–9, 41, 42
as social stratification, 2, 11, 36, 88,
113–14
in status, 36–8, 46, 87, 130
in wealth, 36–9, 41, 42, 46, 88, 109–10,
113, 127, 130
integration, 68
interaction spheres, 6–7, 20, 42, 121–2

Iroquois, 35, 39
Izapa, 123, 124

Jerusalem, 66
Johnson, Allen W., 134
Johnson, Gregory, 134
Joyce, Arthur, 29

kinship, *see* descent groups
Kirkby, Anne, 25
Kowalewski, Stephen A., 24, 133, 134

Laguna Zope, 124, 125
languages
in Mesoamerica, 9
in Oaxaca, 29
La Venta, 123, 124

Marcus, Joyce, 23, 133, 134
markets, *see* exchange of goods
Markman, Charles W., 25
Marx, Karl, 113, 134
Maya region, 1, 9, 11–12, 21, 23, 123,
125, 128, 129
Mazaltepec, Santo Tomás, 82–3, 122, 127
Mesoamerica, 1, 7–20, 40, 41, 77, 118,
119, 126, 129
Mesopotamia, 1, 113, 116
Miahuatlán Valley, 25, 31, 91, 94
Middle Formative period, 42–7
migration, 6, 15, 52, 53, 54, 55, 108
Mixe, 25, 29, 41, 64
Mixtec, 23, 25, 29
Mixteca Alta, 29, 122, 123, 124, 125,
126
moiety, 39–42, 130
Monte Albán, 1, 3, 22, 26–7, 34, 46,
48–67, 132, 134
barrio subdivisions in, 61
external relations of, 66–7, 121–7
Main Plaza of, 22, 61–2, 128
mapping of, 24, 51
origins of, 48–67, 130
Period I population estimates for, 53
as regional capital, 49–66
regional role of, 62–3, 82, 89–94, 100,
107–10, 119
rulers of, 128–9

Nakbe, 125
Natchez chiefdom, 37
network polities, 129
New Delhi, 65–6
New Guinea, 39
Nochixtlán Valley, 25, 122
Northwest coast societies, 35, 39

6084